The Structure of Religion

Judaism and Christianity

William J. Leffler, II
Paul H. Jones

UNIVERSITY PRESS OF AMERICA,® INC.
Lanham • Boulder • New York • Toronto • Oxford

Copyright © 2005 by
University Press of America,® Inc.
4501 Forbes Boulevard
Suite 200
Lanham, Maryland 20706
UPA Acquisitions Department (301) 459-3366

PO Box 317
Oxford
OX2 9RU, UK

Library of Congress Control Number: 2005928414
ISBN 0-7618-3315-3 (paperback : alk. ppr.)

Contents

Introduction

In inter-religious discussions between Christians and Jews, there is often an underlying response among participants: "We do it the right way. Why do those 'confused' or 'ignorant' people do it differently?"

The authors of this book assume that most people are informed and intelligent, and that the differences between how these two religions function are a direct consequence of their specific "Structures."

This book is the result of many years in which Rabbi William Leffler tried to explain to predominately Christian laypeople how Judaism functions—not the differences in belief but the manifestations which occur. No matter how hard he tried, he would come away from each session with the distinct impression that his audiences did not understand what he was trying to explain. As a rabbi, he could not assume that he did not know what he was talking about, but then neither could he assume that those to whom he was speaking were "confused" or "ignorant." As he contemplated this recurring dilemma, he realized that he had an underlying communication problem. He was talking in a Jewish frame of reference while his audiences were listening in a Christian frame of reference. Because his descriptions and explanations about his religion were unfamiliar to them, and they interpreted them through Christian lenses, his listeners just did not understand. Although they were knowledgeable about their religion, they were captive to their particular Christian presuppositions about the meaning and function of religion. They could not escape this "box" because their experience in inter-religious dialogue was limited. They were simply not accustomed to considering a non-Christian religion as equally valid as their own. As a result, they had great difficulty comprehending how Judaism functions. Once Rabbi Leffler realized this fundamental problem, he began thinking about how to address this communication impasse so that in his explanations of how Judaism functions in comparison to Christianity, he might be both heard and understood by his Christian audiences.

Through a process of reflection and refinement he developed the Structure of Religion, which constitutes the first part of this book. By using this Structure, he found that he could both overcome more easily the communication problems that he had experienced and explain more effectively how Judaism functions.

However, to his pleasant surprise, as he began to use the Structure, he soon realized that it worked for both Judaism and Christianity. That is, it can be employed to illustrate Christian manifestations for Jews, as well as Jewish ones for Christians. He further found that through the use of the Structure, when the manifestations of one of the religions were seen in comparison with similar or dissimilar manifestations of the other religion, that many of the topics which he was presenting made much more sense when they were addressed together rather than when they were viewed in isolation. Thus, he discovered that he was able to explain more successfully to Christian audiences the manifestations of Judaism which had puzzled his earlier groups, as well as compare the differences between the two religions not in terms of theological distinctions but in terms of actual behavior, which are the true stumbling blocks to inter-religious understanding. Likewise, Jews were not only more easily able to understand how Christianity functions, but also to see how their own religion functions, in ways that they already knew but frequently could not explain to non-Jews when asked to do so.

Thus, the Structure of Judaism enabled Christians to compare Judaism with similar, and even dissimilar, manifestations found within their own tradition, and for Jews to do the same. Rabbi Leffler could point out to his audiences, both Christian and Jewish, that many of the illustrations which he was using were not new to them, but rather that they had never thought about them in the way in which the Structure explains them. Because the Structure worked, it made his task much easier. We believe that it will work for you also, clarifying many of the "mysteries" which have confounded Christian observers of Judaism, as well as for Jews who have tried to understand why Christians behave as they do.

In the mid-1980s, Professor Paul H. Jones, then Dean of the Chapel at Transylvania University in Lexington, Kentucky, met Rabbi Leffler. After he described the Structure to Professor Jones, they agreed that this way of understanding the two religions was an ideal topic for Jones' undergraduate survey course on Judaism and Christianity. Rabbi Leffler lectured to Dr. Jones' class, and as they say, "the rest is history." Rabbi Leffler has returned annually to teach the class about the Structure of Religion. This presentation has proven to be quite stimulating for each year's class, as well as for both Bill and Paul—by now close personal friends.

Bill had wanted to write a book describing the Structure for many years, but was delayed for a host of reasons. In the year 2000, however, he approached Paul about co-authoring this book, since he was both familiar with the Structural approach and could bring a necessary Christian perspective to the project. Paul agreed and they began to develop the chapters which are in this book—both the six chapters explaining the Structure itself, as well as the subsequent questions for discussion that follow.

While the Structure itself will be new to most readers, we believe that many of the illustrations will be familiar. However, their employment to clarify the Structure may prove unfamiliar since it will require the reader to think outside of his usual religious "box," as previously mentioned. The concept of a religious "box" derives from the realization that most people are socialized into a particular way of understanding through a specific religious tradition. This process of initiation and inculcation is both necessary and desirable for the formation of a religious identity. Although it is exceedingly demanding, it can be infinitely rewarding for the person in that tradition.

However, a person's religious "box" can also create unanticipated and unacknowledged barriers to communication. We often encounter them when an adherent of one religious tradition imposes his presuppositions about how a religious tradition should think and act onto another religious tradition. Such a reaction creates miscommunication at best and disrespect at worst: miscommunication because the other tradition can never fully disclose its distinctive way of "living in the world" outside of the viewer's "box" and disrespect because the other tradition is never perceived as an "authentic" or "valid" religious expression. Humans, by definition, require socially constructed "boxes." We cannot negotiate the world without cultural and religious orientations or ways of living. However, these requisite lenses can blind us to the legitimacy of alternative ways of religious life in the world. "My way is the only way to be religious" is often a difficult attitude to overcome, and unexpected challenges may be experienced as a threat rather than an occasion for new insights.

Consequently, we believe that genuine communication, understanding, and respect occur when we acknowledge the existence of our own particular religious "biases," as well as the "biases" of the other group. Our use of the term "bias" is descriptive and not a value judgment.

Although learning about the Structure of Religion as presented in this book may at first seem artificial, or even disrespectful of one or the other tradition, our purpose is to advance the process of inter-religious understanding by describing the Jewish and Christian Structures without absolutizing either one.

We hope that the questions in part two, which follow the Structural presentation in part one, will fill in some of the gaps that the Structure does not cover. Moreover, we hope that both sections of this book, when taken together, will provide the basis for greater understanding of the two religions, not just of the beliefs that separate them (which is the subject of countless books) but also of the fundamental reasons for the differences in attitudes and behaviors. We trust that this book will shed new light on the old, and seemingly formidable, barriers that have precluded genuine understanding as well as respect between Jews and Christians.

We also need to mention that for ease of reading we have consistently used the third person singular masculine pronoun "he." To do otherwise we found too disruptive to the flow of the text. Furthermore, the reader will notice that we continually refer back to features of the Structure as we present our numerous descriptions of how it functions. Acknowledging this deliberate style, we believe that it is necessary in order to insure that the reader recognizes each connection to the Structure as we present it.

Our basic premise is this: the vast majority of Jews and Christians are informed and intelligent. The differences between how they function within their own religious traditions, which may initially appear confusing, make sense when seen through the lens of the Structure of Religion. It is our fervent hope that this book will contribute to the necessary task of identifying and removing many of the barriers in inter-religious dialogues among laypersons, as well as scholars, which have confounded people of good will over the years.

We conclude the introduction by acknowledging the people who have assisted with the preparation of this manuscript. To President Charles Shearer and Deans James Moseley, David Shannon, and William Pollard of Transylvania University we extend our special appreciation for their encouragement. Support from the Kenan Sabbatical Support Fund and the David and Betty Jones Faculty Development Fund were most helpful. Turner West, a Transylvania University graduate, assisted with the index. To the many people who heard and commented on our various presentations of the Structure—especially the countless church and synagogue study groups and the many religion classes at Transylvania University—we express our gratitude for their thoughtful responses. We are also most grateful to Rabbis Frank Sundheim, Larry Mahrer, and Simeon Maslin, who have used the Structure in their presentations to Christian groups and found that the Structure has made their interpretive task so much easier. And most important, in sincere and deep affection for their love and understanding, we dedicate this book to our wives, Ki Leffler and Merry Jones.

Part One

THE STRUCTURE

Chapter One

Two Christian Myths about Judaism

The historical relationship between Judaism and Christianity has been troubled at best and tragic at worst. The often bloodstained history of Jewish-Christian relations begins in the first century of the Common Era.[1] As Christianity developed its separate identity apart from Judaism, Jewish-Christian relations gradually polarized, as illustrated by chapter nine, verse twenty-two of the Gospel of John written around 90 C.E.: "His parents said this because they were afraid of the Jews, for the Jews had already agreed that anyone who confessed Jesus to be the Messiah would be put out of the synagogue."[2] Thus, some passages in the Christian New Testament, written during this period when Christianity was still understood by many to be a Jewish sect, reflect a strong antipathy towards the Jews and the Judaism of that time. (Although most of the New Testament writers were Jewish, the apparent anti-Jewish pronouncements in the text were later used to justify the church's historic prejudice against Judaism.)

Subsequently, Christianity claimed that it was the "true" religion. God had now rejected historic Judaism and its ancient covenant. Furthermore, Christians interpreted the Jewish Bible in a way that predicted Jesus as the Messiah, and therefore they proclaimed that Christianity superseded Judaism. Jews were still the "chosen people" of old but this privileged status was negated by their deliberate and willful rejection of Jesus. Thus, the rationale for the historic mistreatment of Jews and Judaism emerged because God, according to Christian teaching, had abandoned them.

The Christian hatred of the Jews as unbelievers reached theological maturity during the medieval period when the formal charge of "deicide"—killers of Christ and thus God incarnate—evolved. Jews were now officially cast by the church as the villains in God's drama of salvation and in their misery they witnessed to the triumph of Christianity.

3

And what the church confirmed in theology, it enacted in history. During the Crusades and the Inquisition, Jews were massacred by the thousands and ghettoes were plundered with the blessing of both religious and civil authorities.

The legitimization of anti-Judaism, which became anti-Semitism in modern times, reached its heinous peak with the "final solution" under Adolf Hitler and the Third Reich. Beginning with the loss of basic human rights for Jews, this systematic purge, which was supported by the German state church, culminated in the death of six million Jews, in addition to more than six million other Europeans. However, the Jews were singled out for genocide for no other reason than that they were Jewish.

TWO MYTHS

In *A Short History of Judaism*,[3] Jacob Neusner identifies two Christian myths about Judaism that serve as the intellectual foundations of this religiously based antagonism. Propagated through the centuries and still preached from the pulpits of many Christian churches, these misinterpretations continue to nurture anti-Judaism among both the laity and the learned. Before any serious study of the Structure of Judaism and Christianity can proceed, these inaccuracies must be recognized, discussed, and refuted.

First Myth: Judaism is Christianity without Christ

Many Christians perceive Judaism not as a religion in its own right but as Christianity without Christ. That is, Judaism is an underdeveloped form of Christianity at best, and a deeply flawed form of Christianity at worst, since it rejects Jesus as the Messiah. The first interpretation views Judaism as the religion of "the Old Testament" (note the Christian bias in the juxtaposition between "old" and "new" testaments, see part two, a Christian response to question six) and therefore reads the Jewish Bible (Old Testament) through the lens of the New Testament (see a Christian response to question seven). The second interpretation vitiates the legitimacy of Judaism and therefore leads to an aggressive evangelization of Jews so that they too can experience the salvation Christians know in Jesus the Christ. Although these two positions vary in style, degree, and substance, they share a common assumption: both focus almost exclusively on the Jewish "no" to Jesus and therefore woefully neglect the prior Jewish "yes" to God as revealed in the Hebrew Bible and which Jews believe is still operative.

Although the complex and convoluted historical relationship between Judaism and Christianity should not be oversimplified, there is an historical explanation for this myth. According to Gabriele Boccaccini, Professor of New Testament and Second Temple Judaism at the University of Michigan, in his article "Multiple Judaisms," in the February 1995 issue of *Bible Review*, Christians and Jews alike have both adopted an inadequate model to interpret their shared heritage coming from the period of the incipient church and the development of Rabbinic Judaism. The traditional model views Pharisaic Judaism (as reflected in the Gospels) as the normative Judaism of the late Second Temple period (the time of Jesus). Regrettably, this interpretation overlooks the rich diversity of Judaism of that era. Such a view presents the Essenes (associated with Qumran and the Dead Sea Scrolls), the Sadducees (associated with the Second Temple), and the other forms of Judaism as simply lesser sects. This perception has served the needs of both religious communities for too long. For Jews, this model emphasizes "their enduring fidelity to an ancient and unaltered tradition." For Christians, this model emphasizes "the absolute newness and uniqueness of Jesus of Nazareth" and therefore reinforces the conviction that Christianity replaced an ancient, outdated religion.

But since the late 1940s, with the discovery of the Dead Sea Scrolls and other Second Temple manuscripts, a new model has gradually evolved. Instead of interpreting Judaism as monolithic and static, scholars now see it as dynamic and developing over time. Succinctly, the destruction of Jerusalem and the Second Temple by the Romans in 70 C.E. precipitated a substantive change in Jewish religious practice. Without the Temple, priests, and the sacrificial system Judaism had to reconstitute itself. This unprecedented period of religious identity crisis for Judaism parallels the emergence of the fledgling group of Jewish followers of Jesus. (Most scholars date the New Testament writings from approximately 50–100 C.E., with the Gospels composed between 70–100 C.E.) Hence, the formation of both historic Judaism (Pharisaic Judaism which survived as Rabbinic Judaism) and Christianity (that took some aspects of Pharisaic Judaism) *occurred simultaneously*. Thus, Christianity incorporated elements of Rabbinic Judaism within itself, especially the mode of worship found in the synagogue and the citation of Biblical verses (technically called "proof texting") to support theological ideas.

Historians now know of only two forms of Judaism that survived after 70 C.E. Both Rabbinic Judaism and the Jesus movement proceeded along different paths and therefore jockeyed for dominance during the second half of the first century of the Common Era. Since Neusner understands any religious system that appeals "as an important part of its authoritative literature or canon to the Hebrew Scriptures of ancient Israel" to be Jewish, both Rabbinic Judaism and Christianity qualify.

Consequently, this new model declares both Rabbinic Judaism and Christianity as legitimate heirs of post-Second Temple Judaism. The rabbis, associated with the synagogue, shared their survival with another group of Jews that history now designates as Christians. In short, the emergence of Rabbinic Judaism as the normative form of post-Second Temple Judaism does not deprive Christianity of its Jewish roots any more than the birth of Christianity deprives Judaism of its legitimacy.

The realization that Rabbinic Judaism and Christianity share a common heritage affords an equally significant shift at the level of root metaphor. Viewed as two distinct religions, the prior model invoked the familial relationship of parent-child to characterize the historical relationship between Judaism and Christianity. As the parent, Judaism birthed Christianity. And by inference, the child, Christianity, superceded the parent, resulting in the myth of Judaism as a form of Christianity without Christ.

Scholars now understand that the new model perceives Rabbinic Judaism and Christianity as born "of the same womb," i.e., the historic period when Jerusalem and the Temple were destroyed. Consequently, the more accurate root metaphor is "fraternal twins." Although both religions emerged in the same historic context and responded to the same set of identity and survival questions, they offered different visions of how post-Second Temple Judaism should evolve.

Most important, according to Alan Segal, professor of religion at Barnard College, Columbia University, the "time of Jesus marks the beginning of not one but two great religions of the West, Rabbinic Judaism and Christianity . . . As brothers often do, they picked different, even opposing ways to preserve their family's heritage."[4] While Rabbinic Judaism claims that it has honored the traditions of Israel by following the dual Torah tradition (the Written Torah or Scripture, and the Oral Torah or Rabbinic literature, principally the Talmud), Christianity maintains that it alone is the new Israel (since Christ is the second Adam). According to the new model, both affirmations are correct. Rabbinic Judaism and Christianity are different Jewish responses to the demise of the Judaism of the post-Biblical period and the crisis engendered by the destruction of Jerusalem and the Second Temple.

Second Myth: Judaism is Not a Valid Religion

The second myth often expressed by Christians is that Judaism is no longer a valid religion. This misperception is a natural and logical extension of the first myth. In his excellent book, *The Jews in the Time of Jesus*, Rabbi Stephen Wylen correctly states, the "Jews of today, like . . . Christians, wish to be acknowledged as believers in a separate and distinct religion that is complete in itself. Each religion has its own integrity. The ultimate goal is not merger but mutual respect."[5] In order to achieve "mutual respect," a person first needs to understand his own religion and why it behaves as it does before he can begin to comprehend the ways of another religion. This is not easy. We all tend to assume that every religion reflects the thought patterns and behaviors of our own religion. Such a presumption, however, presents a major stumbling block.

This second myth elicits a basic question for the Christian: Is Judaism still a valid Religion? The question appears to be a straightforward, simple one to the Christian who asks it. However, it is really a very difficult and confusing question for a number of reasons, as we shall illustrate. By contrast, a Jew seldom asks such a question. He generally knows that Judaism is still a valid religion, though at times he may not be too sure why it is or even how to explain what he means by that word to a non-Jew. It is this difference in understanding of what is meant by "religion" that is the basis for the confusion which occurs and why we need to address it—especially at the beginning of a book comparing the two religions. An awareness of some crucial differences in the understanding of the word "religion" between Christians and Jews is fundamental to an understanding of the differences in the manifestations and behavior between the two "religions." To reiterate, the text of this book will not address any of the theological differences which occur. Our focus is on differences in behavior and manifestation, for these are what more often pose the problems in inter-religious dialogues and in the efforts to develop good relationships.

The basic reason for the question "Is Judaism a Religion?" (not just a "valid" one) is that in ordinary usage the Christian tends to use the word "religion" synonymously with "faith" or "belief." This is how most Westerners understand the word. We speak about inter-faith activities when we mean inter-religious activities. We refer to matters of belief and faith when we discuss aspects of theology that we think are central to religion. These assumptions are reinforced by the dictionary when it includes among its numerous definitions of "religion" phrases like "true believers," "systems of faith," "religious beliefs," and "religious faith." We are so accustomed to using the word "religion" in this fashion that we tend to overlook any other meaning. Yet when we encounter Judaism, these assumptions about the meaning of "religion" do not work. Judaism appears to be a "religion" which is far more than just a matter of what one believes or one's faith. But the Christian knows no other reference point by which to interpret Judaism. As a result, confusion occurs.

The question is further exacerbated when we examine what a number of scholars say about their understanding of the word "religion." Robert Speer, a Presbyterian ecumenist and prolific author, maintains that (his own) Christianity "is not a religion" at all, but rather "good news from God." John MacMurray, one of the twentieth century's most famous philosophers, declares that "the moment Christianity becomes a religion it ceases to be Christianity." Additionally he points out that the word "religion" does not occur even once in any of the Four Gospels, and neither is it found in the Hebrew Bible. Rabbi Mordecai Kaplan calls Judaism a "religious civilization" and insists that it could be better understood in sociological terms rather than in the usual theological terms. A number of Jewish thinkers have characterized Judaism as a "Way of Life," a designation that far exceeds what we normally consider a "religion" to be. Moreover, there are other scholars who openly declare that religion is an indefinable word. Thus, among both Christian and Jewish scholars there are many who would not only question the commonly held assumptions that the dictionary reflects, but who also find these assumptions to be inaccurate and inadequate for their respective religion.

Nonetheless, in general conversation most people continue to assume that religion = faith = belief. Thus, we need to ask: Why does this occur? It is really very simple. Our everyday English usage of the word "religion" evolved from the British who were Christian and therefore devised their religious language to meet their Christian presuppositions and needs. Because a person becomes a Christian by affirming one's belief in Christ or one's faith in Christ, the English language reflects this assumption. These three words (religion, faith, belief) are now so closely associated within Christianity — in its worship service, its creedal and theological statements of belief, and the way in which Christians talk about their religion — that most people in our culture naturally assume that this linguistic equation fits all religions, including Judaism (see a Christian response to question four).

But additional problems occur, even within Christianity. They happen because Christianity also has within it moral principles, teachings about how the adherent should behave in any given situation. Many of these revolve around the Ten Commandments, as reflected by the efforts of some well intended Christians to place these Biblical laws on the walls in public school classrooms and judicial chambers. Christian moral standards enter the debate on abortion, with both sides questioning the sincerity, and even the legitimacy, of the opinions of those who differ with them. The debate over the use of the death penalty and the "just war" theory also encompass moral standards. These and many other instances in which behavior or ethical principles are invoked clearly indicate that what one believes about Christ is not the only criterion by which to ascertain whether a person is or is not a Christian, or perhaps even a "good" Christian. Thus, a cursory look at how Christianity functions indicates that the equation (religion=faith=belief) has additional difficulties. Nonetheless, while appropriate behavior is certainly central to being a Christian, it is faith and belief, as we shall point out, that is the starting place for Christianity.

JUDAISM AND THE DEFINITION OF RELIGION

The problem of defining the word "religion" becomes even more complicated when we address Judaism, and which brings us back once more to our question: "Is Judaism a religion?" The simple answer is "yes." However, there are a number of important qualifications.

First, we need to consider two ancillary questions: "Is Judaism a race?" "Is Judaism a nationality?" Both are legitimate queries. And both receive the same response: "No"—but often a very confused "No." Why? This occurs because these questions identify an unexpressed but general assumption shared by our society when comparisons between groups are made. For example, the underlying meaning of the terms Latino, Blacks, and Jews differs. The first is a reference to an individual or his family's geographic place of origin; the second refers to a racial background; the third refers to a religious people. These examples reflect three different kinds of identities, yet they are often unreflectively used side-by-side. We blur the distinctions and muddy our understanding of the categorical differences when they are used in this way.

We find an illustration of this confusion in *The Half-Jewish Book*[6] by Daniel Klein and Freke Viujst in which the authors discuss the situations of people who have one parent who is Jewish and one parent who is "something other." While the book often cites individuals with one Jewish and one Christian parent, which is a difference in religion, it also identifies people who are "half Jewish/half African American," or who are half-Jewish and half-Mohawk or half- Irish, as if being Jewish is not only a religious identity, but also a racial or national identity as well. Thus, this book, which is full of examples of well-known people who have one Jewish parent and therefore are "half-Jewish," is an excellent illustration of the confusion that occurs over whether Judaism is a "religion" or whether it is something other. Apparently, the authors of this book never asked themselves or the people about whom they wrote, the fundamental question which we believe is essential for an understanding of Judaism on its own terms: Is Judaism a religion? As further illustration of this difficulty, no one ever says that someone is "half-Christian" if he has one Christian parent. Such a category makes no sense, which is why people do not use it.

A second illustration of this confusion is found in Michele Guinness' book, *A Little Kosher Seasoning*.[7] Guinness is a British woman who was born a Jew, converted to Christianity as a teenager, and subsequently married an

Anglican clergyman. Her book attempts to convey to her Christian readers (among whom are her own children) an understanding of Jewish life through a discussion of holiday observances and rituals. While her intention is admirable, that of increasing the reader's understanding of her former religion so that they can add some Jewish insights to their practice of Christianity, her attempt to synthesize the two religions inevitably fails. Although her book may help those who are not in her immediate family, to her children she is and will always be a Christian. Therefore the understandings she wishes to impart to them about her former religion, Judaism, will be preserved merely as a family memory, both for them and for their children. They are Christians who happen to have a mother who was born a Jew and became a Christian.

A third illustration of this category confusion is the United Nations General Assembly Resolution 3379 of November 10, 1975, which in part "condemned Zionism as a threat to world peace and security, and called upon all countries to oppose this racist . . . ideology." Zionism, which led to the establishment of the State of Israel in 1948, comes out of a religion, Judaism, not out of a racial group. Such a misbegotten declaration by the United Nations only adds confusion to the subject.

Is Judaism a Race?

We are now ready to address more fully the confusion found in the UN resolution, by asking: "Is Judaism a race?"

On the one hand, people cannot convert from or into a race, even though the authors of the book about "half-Jews" seem to indicate that Judaism is somehow a "race." The UN resolution, mentioned above, reflects the same confusion. Obviously one cannot say that next week I shall become Black, or White, or Native American or Asian, all of which are racial groupings. It is just not possible. On the other hand, there are people who do convert to Judaism, who forsake their prior religion for whatever reason and decide to become Jewish. In the same way, there are Jews who do not wish to remain Jews and convert to another religion. As further illustration of this state of confusion, the Union for Reform Judaism (formerly the Union of American Hebrew Congregations), the national organization of Reform synagogues, in the fall 2001 issue of its magazine *Reform Judaism*, fell into this trap by advertising on its cover an article within it dealing with intermarriage whose headline read: "50% (of those Jews polled) think it's racist to oppose mixed marriages (with non-Jews)." Judaism simply is not a "race," and for a Jewish organization to use such terms obfuscates rather then enlightens, and shows the extent of the confusion on this question, even within a national Jewish organization.

Historically, this confusion dates to the Spanish Inquisition. Although many Jews converted to Catholicism and were baptized, they were still perceived suspiciously. Therefore, an additional reason was invented to legitimize persecution after baptism. Spanish Inquisitors imposed the category of "blood" or race onto the "New Christians"—later called "Marranos," often thought to mean "pigs." The new legal barriers excluded anyone from certain positions of power "who did not have the requisite *limpieza de sangre* or 'purity of blood.'"[8] Finally, it was Adolf Hitler who solidified in the modern era the association of "race" and Jews when he justified the Final Solution on racial grounds. Douglas Rushkoff, author of *Nothing Sacred: The Truth About Judaism*, in an address to the Jewish Outreach Institute Board of Directors on March 10, 2003, asserted: "So the Jews, who were originally persecuted for their refusal to submit to the artificial racial and theistic boundaries of their contemporaries, now thought of themselves as a race, too."[9]

We shall return to this topic in later chapters.

Is Judaism a Nationality?

Similarly, Judaism is not a nationality, even though many Jews today reside in the modern State of Israel. Historically, the last independent Jewish state of ancient times ceased to exist after the Roman conquest of Palestine in 63 B.C.E.[10] by General Pompey. Prior to that period, however, Jews had already begun to move out of that geographic area and had become residents of Babylonia, Rome, Alexandria, and many of the other important communities of the ancient Mediterranean basin. The Diaspora ("scattering") had begun. Since that time, and until 1948, there was no Jewish state. Although many of the Eastern European peoples during the rise of modern nationalism viewed Jews living in their midst as part of another nation, until the appearance of the State of Israel, Jews had no nationality other than that of the geographic areas in which they resided. As a religion, Judaism has centuries of historic memory, similar to a nation state. Nonetheless, in modern times, even with the establishment of the State of Israel, the majority of Jews do not live there but remain citizens of their countries of residence.

Is Judaism a Religion?

We return now to our primary question, "Is Judaism a religion?" We have said "yes," but with qualifications. Let us now consider the first part of our response, since this locates the point of confusion. The "yes" focuses our attention on the use of the word "religion" in English as we have already mentioned. This usage developed to meet Christian presuppositions about what religion entails, and, as indicated above, it provides a fairly adequate under-standing of the word in common parlance. However, our problem is that an English understanding of this word, as we have come to accept it, is totally inadequate for an understanding of Judaism as a "religion." It simply does not work! Just as Christianity is not Judaism, neither does the Christian use of the word "religion" prove adequate for an understanding of Judaism. This differ-ence may startle those Christians who have not encountered an alternative un-derstanding of the word "religion." This is often the case with Jews, too. Not only are Jews socialized into the dominant (read Christian) use of the term "religion," but more importantly Judaism does not systematically define its beliefs. It talks about religious ideas, since neither modern nor historical Jew-ish literature methodically defines its terms. Consequently, Douglas Rushkoff describes Judaism as more of a religion about "process" and "ideas" than "a thing one 'believes' in."[11]

Because of this difference, the Jewish use of the word "religion" has a far broader meaning than what is generally understood from its common English usage, even though it certainly does contain elements of faith and belief as in Christianity. But neither of those words is adequate to convey what Judaism encompasses. It is far more than just a "faith" or a "religion" with a creedal statement of "belief."

Judaism involves three dimensions of life that are so intertwined that it is not possible to separate them. These three aspects of life are: People, Ideas, and Behavior.

People

Judaism is the religion of an ancient group of people, the historically trace-able descendants of those Israelites who stood at the base of Mount Sinai in the time of Moses and said "yes" to God. In religious terms, God made a covenant with this people to be their God and for them to be God's people. The Hebrew word for this covenant is *B'rit*, or *B'ris*, or *B'rith*, depending on the pronunciation of the language which one chooses. However, whichever pronunciation one uses, Jews continue to hold that that centuries-old covenant is still operative and in place, neither superseded by Christian claims nor substituted for another. The word is still very much present in Jew-ish usage today. The name for the ritual circumcision of an eight-day-old male is *B'rit Milah*, the covenant of circumcision. The Jewish fraternal or-ganization is *B'nai B'rith* (literally "Sons of the Covenant"). Many syna-gogues employ this word in their title, e.g., *B'rit Emet* (Covenant of Truth) or *B'rit Shalom* (Covenant of Peace). Only a viable people could have gone back to Palestine, the land of its origins, after an absence of almost two millennia and establish the modern State of Israel. When one reads the liturgy of the synagogue in the prayer book, the Jewish People, liturgically referred to as "Israel," is prominent in the prayers. The historic Jewish People is central to Judaism as a religion. As Rabbi David Wolpe, of Los Angeles, has written, "Judaism is like a tribe, or a family." And Professor Jacob Neusner, in an article in the May 8, 2002 issue of the *Jewish Post and Opinion*, reiterates this same awareness: "Jews who practice Judaism always belong to the ethnic group, the Jews," whether by birth or by conversion.

Ideas

There is far more to Judaism than just a People. Judaism includes religious ideas. Axiomatic is the ancient belief in one God (monotheism). On one level, the Hebrew Bible narrates the encounter of the Jewish People with their God, who evolved from the God of a family—Abraham, Isaac and Jacob—into eventually becoming a universal God, concerned for all of humanity. In Jack Miles' book, *God: A Biography*,[12] this covenantal relationship is superbly described and developed. The Bible also speaks about the need for this People to sanctify life, to be holy as their God is holy (Leviticus 19), and to live in a way pleasing in God's sight. The literary prophets repeatedly and profoundly remind this People (and us) of that message. Prophetic exhortations about compassion, justice, charity, mercy, and love permeate the text. These religious ideas are integral to the religion of this People, as they are in most all historic religions. David S. Ariel, in his book *What Do Jews Believe*,[13] states, "Judaism is not a religion of fixed doctrines or dogmas but a complex system of evolving beliefs."

Behavior

Behavior is also an essential part of Judaism. Jewish behavior includes many ritual activities, among which are the celebration of holidays and Jewish life cycle events. It also encompasses in specific ways the implementation of many of the religious ideas found in Judaism—caring for the orphan and the widow, being honest in one's business practices, being part of a Minyan (the ten adult males needed for a public worship service), keeping some or all of the Jewish dietary laws, and studying Jewish texts in a Jewish setting. In order for Judaism to be a meaningful religion on a daily basis, Jews put these ideas into practice, through what is called *Halachah* (literally the "Way" in which one should live). That is what it means to be Jewish, from a behavioral standpoint.

CONCLUSION

Thus, Judaism must be understood as a "religion" in a much broader sense than Christianity—as a system of "faith" or "belief." To limit one's understanding to the commonly accepted English usage of the word as found in a dictionary fails to include the breadth of what Judaism encompasses. To invoke the conventional usage of the term "religion" only confuses the Christian, as well as the Jew, who wishes to compare the two religions. Hence, the Christian understanding of "religion" is too restrictive and limiting. Its continued use contributes to the confusion that frequently pervades many inter-religious discussions.

This difficulty is perhaps best illustrated by asking the question, what makes a person a Jew? More often than not the response is likely to be "the belief in one God." For the Christian, this makes sense. He is accustomed to believing in a Trinitarian view of God and, therefore, thinks of Judaism as retaining a Unitarian view of God. That is, Judaism is Christianity without Christ (and the Holy Spirit)—our first myth! However, a non-Trinitarian response might also encompass the Unitarian, the Deist and the general Monotheist, all of whom proclaim a similar, non-Trinitarian belief about God. Not surprisingly, Jews frequently respond in the same way as their Christian neighbors, that he is a Jew because he believes that God is one and not three-in-one. This usually occurs because they are so accustomed to thinking of what religion entails in Christian terms, that they do not stop to think about the question as we have been considering it. However, when Jews are further questioned about their own religion, they will readily admit that they somehow realized the inadequacy of that answer but that they did not know what else to say. On a gut level, most Jews know that Judaism as a religion encompasses a great deal more than just belief, but have never really considered how to move beyond such a limited awareness.

The identification and examination of the two Christian myths about Judaism pinpoint one source of inter-religious misperceptions and misunderstandings. The first myth that Judaism is Christianity without Christ is historically incorrect. Both Rabbinic Judaism and Christianity are different Jewish responses to the destruction of Jerusalem and the Second Temple by the Romans in 70 C.E. Consequently, the emergence of Rabbinic Judaism as the normative form of post-Second Temple Judaism does not deprive Christianity of its Jewish roots any more than the birth of Christianity deprives Judaism of its legitimacy.

The second myth that Judaism is not a valid religion, or even a religion, is functionally incorrect. Because Christians usually impose their preconceived notions of what a "religion" should be (religion=faith=belief) onto Judaism, this confusion continues to exist. The Christian use of the term "religion" proves inadequate for an understanding of Judaism since the latter is more than just a "faith" or a "religion" with a creedal statement of "belief." Our premise is that Judaism necessarily includes three inseparable components: People, Ideas, and Behavior, and is a valid religion for Jews.

Greater insight into these historically related but distinct religions requires a thorough analysis of the underlying structure of each. Only after Judaism and Christianity are seen on their own terms through the Structure of Religion will less confusion and more clarity emerge. In chapter two we present the specifics of the Structure of Religion, an approach to understanding both Judaism and Christianity as each religion functions in the lives of their adherents today.

NOTES

1. This neutral designation (C.E.) replaces the usage of *anno Domini* (A.D.), in the year of our Lord in the Christian era.

2. Unless otherwise designated, all Bible translations are from the New Revised Standard Version (NRSV).

3. See Jacob Neusner, *A Short History of Judaism* (Minneapolis: Fortress Press, 1992), 8 & 212–213.

4. Gabriele Boccaccini, "Multiple Judaisms," *Bible Review* (February 1995): 41.

5. Stephen Wylen, *The Jews in the Time of Jesus* (New York: Paulist Press, 1996), 196.

6. Daniel Klein and Freke Viujst, *The Half-Jewish Book* (New York: Villard, 2000).

7. Michele Guinness, *A Little Kosher Seasoning* (London: Hodder & Stoughton, 1994).

8. Marc Saperstein, *Moments of Crisis in Jewish-Christian Relations* (Philadelphia: Trinity Press, 1989), 27.

9. Douglas Rushkoff, "The Medium is the Message: Getting Over Racehood," *Jewish Outreach Institute* (Spring 2003): 3.

10. Before the Common Era (B.C.E.) is the neutral designation that replaces the Christian usage of Before Christ (B.C.).

11. Rushkoff, "The Medium is the Message," 1.

12. Jack Miles, *God: A Biography* (New York: Vintage Books, 1996).

13. David S. Ariel, *What Do Jews Believe* (New York: Schocken, 1995).

Chapter Two

The Structure of
Judaism and Christianity

As previously indicated, most Christians presume that "religion," "faith," and "belief" are synonymous, and that people join a church by a "profession of faith" (usually by assenting to a creedal statement or by affirming a belief in Jesus as the Christ prior to or after Baptism).[1] Therefore, it is only natural for Christians to assume that Judaism functions in the same way, that Jews must accept a set of beliefs in order to be Jewish.

This assumption is incorrect! Historically, there has only been one significant Jewish creedal statement—Maimonides' "Thirteen Cardinal Principles of Faith"—which dates to the late twelfth century. It is found in the traditional Jewish prayer book as a supplemental reading for the daily morning worship service, as well as poetically in the hymn *Yigdal*. However, neither is integral to the service itself. Judaism has no equivalent to a Christian creedal statement of belief that is used as a measure by which a person is considered to be a Jew. Rabbi Wolpe has observed that no statement of a creedal nature "has been successful in establishing itself" within Judaism. Furthermore, within the formal worship service, there is no public, open affirmation or statement of belief. The Jew is present because he is a Jew. What he specifically believes is irrelevant.

This difference between Judaism and Christianity in approach to matters of belief is significant and needs to be understood because it is often a point of confusion for Christians. Church worship, either intentionally or derivatively, seeks to strengthen one's faith and belief in Christ. Both conservative and liberal congregations, through hymns and prayers, scriptural reading and preaching of the Gospel, proclaim the good news of what God has done and is doing for humanity through Christ. Hymns, for example, retell the story and beliefs about Jesus. Prayers conclude with a Christian seal, such as "In Jesus' name we pray" or "In the name of the Father, the Son, and the Holy Spirit." Liturgical churches emphasize the Sacrament of the Eucharist or the receiving of the Lord Jesus under the forms of bread and wine. All of these worship activities identify, transmit, and sustain the fundamental faith and beliefs of the universal church.

In sharp contrast, Jewish worship is not intended to strengthen the worshipper's faith since it is assumed that the congregant's belief does not need this form of reinforcement. Whether accurate or not, it is taken as a given. As we have just stated, the Jewish worshipper is present because he is a Jew, not because of what he "believes" in any sort of theological sense. The Jew does not need to have his or her religious identify regularly reconfirmed through the words of prayer. It is already in place, and as in one of the opening blessings of the morning Reform service, the worshipper thanks God for making him or her a Jew and for crowning "Israel with glory." There is no mention of "faith."

Based on this very brief comparison, and using only the example of worship, we begin the process of explaining how it is that these two world religions function so very differently in the various areas of religious life. The many differences in manifestations and the reasons behind the differences are what need clarification. They will claim our attention in the first part of this book. As previously indicated, these differences can be very confusing unless one first understands the "Structure of Religion" as it relates to both Judaism and Christianity. This chapter presents a structural approach to the two religions that will enable the reader to comprehend more clearly why these differences exist. Typically, the adherent of one religion assumes that his particular religion is both intelligible and coherent even if a participant in the other religion finds it inexplicable and inappropriate. The Structure explains why this occurs.

Consequently, our basic presupposition must be that both Christians and Jews are "sane" and that how their respective religions function makes perfectly good sense to them. Instead of imposing one's own religious presuppositions onto the other person's religion, this method permits the adherent of one religion to understand the thought processes and manifestations of the other religion within its own Structure. This is not an easy task. Again, most of us are so accustomed to thinking within our own mental "boxes" that we really have to stretch to get outside of them, and both acknowledge and accept as legitimate someone else's mental "box." This chapter is intended to introduce the structural approach to the student of comparative religion and to help him to get out of that "box."

THE STRUCTURE

There is a fundamental Structure to religion that both Judaism and Christianity share. In broad generalities these religious structures are very similar. However, in specifics they vary greatly. And unless one can understand these structural differences and accept them as legitimate, a person will neither comprehend the manifestations of the other religion that are puzzling and unfamiliar, nor will he realize how and why they make sense within the Structure in which they occur.

The Structure has four parts: the Individual, the Bridge-Link, the Essential Element (in Latin *sine qua non*), and the Religion. The individual enters into his religion through the Bridge-Link, then proceeds to the Essential Element, and subsequently to the specifics of that particular religion. We now look more closely at these parts to see how each functions in general.

The Four Parts

The Individual: This designation identifies the specific person, who in his "individualness" is not a member of any particular religion.

The Bridge-Link: This term identifies the vehicle that both initiates the process of the Individual self-consciously joining a religion and connects him to the Essential Element of that specific religion.

The Essential Element: This phrase refers to the constitutive, core component of that religion, which if it is removed from that religion no longer exists, though it may still be a religion of some sort.

The Religion: this word identifies the specific religion. For our purposes in this book, it is either Judaism or Christianity.

Above these four basic parts of the Structure, we place *Rays*. These Rays represent aspects and activities of the Religion in which the Individual may participate in order to be recognized as a member of that specific Religion. While the basic Structure remains constant, both the specifics of the terms and the Rays vary significantly between the two Religions and are therefore the primary location of the confusion that occurs in inter-religious understanding between Christians and Jews. However, as we shall demonstrate, for the Individual to function in a meaningful way within his particular Religion, he must participate in the Rays of that Religion. The Rays provide vehicles of inclusion, as well as public affirmation, for one's selection of that Religion. If a person decides not to participate in the activities designated by the Rays then that Individual will most likely be considered an inactive Christian or a peripheral Jew. Unique to Christianity, the refusal to participate at the level of Rays may even jeopardize one's status as a Christian.

RAYS

THE RELIGION

THE ESSENTIAL ELEMENT

THE BRIDGE-LINK

↑

THE INDIVIDUAL

Diagram: The Structure of Religion

THE CHRISTIAN STRUCTURE

Because Christianity pervades our culture (regardless of one's religious affiliation or non-affiliation), we begin with a description of the Structure as it operates in Christianity. First, we need to discern the Christian Bridge-Link by which the Individual moves into the Structure and subsequently into the Christian Religion. From our previous chapter, it should be obvious by now that *Faith-Belief* functions as the *Bridge-Link* that brings the person into a relationship with the Essential Element and then into Christianity. As we have indicated, Christianity places a great emphasis on what one believes. Failure to subscribe to normative standards may cause a person to forfeit his place in the community of faith, that is, to be considered non-Christian by other Christians.

The *Essential Element* for *Christianity* should also be obvious: *Christ*. Without Christ, there is no Christianity as its very name implies. However, most Christian denominations affirm a belief in the Trinity—God, Christ, and the Holy Spirit—and therefore Faith-Belief in Christ alone is usually not sufficient (see part two, a Christian response to question ten). The Essential Element also requires God. However, belief in God alone is not sufficient to be a Christian. As Christian creeds declare, belief in both God and Christ are essential. According to the Apostles' Creed which is widely used in the western churches, Christians "believe in God the Father Almighty . . . and in Christ Jesus, his only son, our Lord." And according to the Nicene Creed which was formulated in 325 C.E. and widely regarded as the basis for orthodox Christianity in both the eastern and western churches, adherents "believe in one God, the Father All-Mighty, maker of all things visible and invisible; And in one Lord Jesus Christ, the Son of God, begotten from the Father, only-begotten, that is, of the substance of the Father . . . ." Thus, the triune structure innate to Christian experience, and therefore Christian belief, mandates that Christ, plus God, be the Essential Element. Hence, *"Christ (God)"* is the designation we shall use.

The Individual, through Faith-Belief in Christ (God), can now enter into his specific Religion, Christianity. But a person must take an additional step in order to be recognized by other Christians as a Christian. The Individual needs to go beyond a "generalized" or "theoretical" acceptance of Christianity and join a community of faith. Thus, the Rays in Christianity (which interestingly may be turned into crosses) are the many different Christian communities—Roman Catholic, Orthodox, Baptist, Presbyterian, Episcopalian, Pentecostal, Disciples of Christ, etc—that one may join in order to indicate what Faith-Belief in Christ means in specific terms. A convert or new adherent to Christianity attests to his or her Christianity in this way. There exists no alternative, for if one decides not to identify with a particular church, other Christians may well question whether that person really is a Christian. The churched Christian cannot be certain that the unchurched Christian really belongs to his Religion. Both the automobile bumper sticker that declares "Join me in Church on Sunday" and the assignment of revival converts to specific churches make this point. Individuals cannot remain "saved" in general terms; they must be referred to a local church congregation to complete the process. The people who claim that they are Christian but do not participate in a church are perceived skeptically by active church members.

Since additional illustrations of specific areas of confusion within the Christian Structure will surface in subsequent chapters, we proceed to a description of the Jewish Structure.

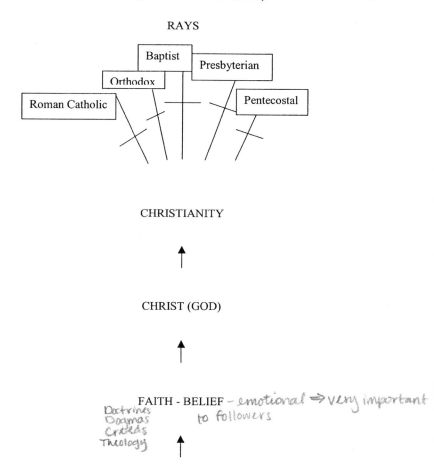

FAITH - BELIEF – *emotional* ⇒ very important
Doctrines   to followers
Dogmas
Creeds
Theology

THE INDIVIDUAL
Diagram: The Christian Structure

THE JEWISH STRUCTURE

Again we start with the Individual, the person who wishes to move into Judaism. Like our treatment of Christianity, the Bridge-Link must be identified in order that the person may encounter the Essential Element of Judaism and thereby enter into this particular religion. Unlike Christianity, the Jewish *Bridge-Link* is not (as many people think) a belief in one God, comparable to the Faith-Belief Bridge-Link of Christianity. As previously mentioned in chapter one, a belief in one God is not sufficient to make a person a Jew. Rather, it is one's *Conscious Self-Identification* as a Jew, an identity that has been learned and acquired from infancy through participation in the Jewish community for the person born a Jew, or that has been developed within himself for the convert. When someone says "Jew," this Individual responds in the first person. That reference is to "me" or to "us."

Consequently, the *Essential Element* in *Judaism* becomes the historic *Jewish People*, the people who stood at the base of Mount Sinai so many centuries ago and said "yes" to God (in whatever interpretation of that event one may choose). They made a covenant to be God's people, that the God of "Abraham, Isaac, and Jacob" would be their God. Judaism is the Religion of this viable and visible group of people throughout the pages of history from that ancient time until the present, and even extending into the future. Regardless of the many changes that have occurred over the centuries (differences effected by time, space, or thought, as well as the spiritual yearnings that it has and will encompass), there is no Judaism without this historic People. Peretz Smolenskin, an early Zionist, wrote in the mid-1870s: "No matter what his sins against religion, every Jew belongs to his people so long as he does not betray it."

However, just as we put God in parenthesis after Christ in Christianity, so too do we need to place God in parenthesis after the Jewish People. God needs to be present as part of the Essential Element in both Religions. For Judaism, it is the *People's relationship to God* that fulfills this role. The exodus from Egypt and the covenant at Mount Sinai underscore this particular and peculiar relationship between God and the Jewish people. Without God, Judaism as a Religion is truncated, even though in today's world we find Jews who are secular and do not include God in their understanding of Judaism. Nonetheless, the complete *Essential Element* is: *the Jewish People (in Relationship to God)*.

And so the Individual, through his Conscious Self-Identification as being a part of this ongoing historic Jewish People (and not simultaneously a part of any other religious tradition, as we shall illustrate later) comes into the Jewish Religion.

And like Christianity, there are Rays above Judaism, manifestations of the Religion in which the Individual may participate. These activities will be addressed in subsequent chapters.

RAYS

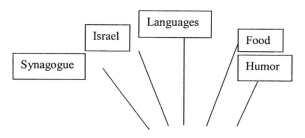

JUDAISM [compare to Faith-Belief p.21]
Religious ideas
non-systematic
Stream of consciousness
assumptive

THE JEWISH PEOPLE
(IN RELATIONSHIP TO GOD)
Israel

CONSCIOUS SELF-IDENTIFICATION

↑

THE INDIVIDUAL
Diagram: The Jewish Structure

CONCLUSION

Our descriptions of the Structure of Religion for both Christianity and Judaism are now complete. Although the general structural components are the same, the specifics by which an Individual enters each Religion are quite different. Whereas the affirmation of a Faith-Belief in Christ (God) is the means by which the Individual becomes a Christian, there is no corresponding Faith-Belief element in the basic structure of Judaism. This does not mean that Faith-Belief is not present or important within Judaism, but rather that it occurs in a very different location within the Structure from where it occurs in Christianity.

The importance of this difference in Structure to an understanding of the attendant differences between Judaism and Christianity cannot be over-emphasized. Since religious differences, and not similarities, are the stumbling blocks, the Structure enables us to pinpoint specific problems and their resolution.

In conclusion, we want to present two illustrations of a difference between these two religions that are reflected in the Structure. First, the history of Judaism chronicles the religion of a specific group of people. There are many books written on this subject—some attempt to cover the entire sweep of Jewish history (from the time of the Bible to the present) while other books address limited topics like the history of a specific Jewish community (perhaps the Jews of America or Germany). These latter tomes focus on the experiences of the People in whatever geographic area the book treats. Or, the book will consider a specific movement within Jewish history, e.g., the role of the Pharisees in the time of the Second Temple period (about 100 B.C.E. to 70 C.E.), or the rise of modern Hasidism. Although the synagogue may be included in these examinations, it is usually a minor aspect of the total experience of the Jews about whom the author writes.

By contrast, a book on Christian history almost always treats the history of the *ecclesia* (the Greek word that means "gathering" and is usually translated as "church"), the religious institution. It may be a history of the development of the early church, or the Protestant Reformation, or even of one of the many modern Christian denominations. But it is not a history of the Christian people per se, in the same way that a history of the Jews, or even one facet of Judaism, would be. This is a significant difference in the nature of any historical study dealing with the two religions, one that is very often not noted but which becomes very obvious when seen through the lens of the Structure of Religion.

The second difference illustrates how the Structure influences the use and interpretation of words. Both religions employ the words "salvation" and "redemption." However, their respective meanings vary greatly. On the one hand, "salvation" is usually associated for Christians with issues of proper Faith-Belief, often related to a concern for life-after-death. Consequently, a major purpose of Christian evangelism is to save souls and insure that the individual has a favorable seat in the hereafter. On the other hand, "redemption" relates to sin. Christ, through his death and resurrection, redeemed humanity from the bondage of sin. Thus, Christian theologians have constructed elaborate atonement theories to explain this cosmic mystery.

By contrast, while Judaism uses both of these words, they do not have the same meaning. Within Jewish thought, "salvation" focuses on this world. The individual is "saved" from a meaningless existence by living as a Jew. Life is sanctified through religious actions, both ritual and ethical. "Redemption" is connected to the exodus from Egypt. God "redeemed" the ancient Hebrews from slavery,[2] and, by extension, Jews hope that God will continue to redeem the Jewish people and, by implication, all the world from the degradation that results from any form of human slavery.[3]

Although both religions employ the same religious terms, the meanings are quite different. They result from the differences in the specific Structures, which in turn produce the distinct manifestations which we shall further consider within this section of the book.

NOTES

1. Because there are over 34,000 Protestant denominations (see part two, a Christian response to questions 8 & 9), it is dubious at best and dangerous at worst to generalize about Christian practices—especially Christian worship. However, most major branches of Christendom practice either infant baptism (during a worship service water is usually sprinkled on the infant before the child is one year of age—practiced by the Orthodox, Roman Catholic, Lutheran, Anglican/Episcopalian, Methodist, and Presbyterian churches) or adult/believers' baptism (during a worship service a person of "age" is immersed in water after making a "profession of faith" in Jesus as their savior—practiced by Baptist, Disciples of Christ, Church of Christ, Independent Christian, Evangelical, and Pentecostal churches). Regardless of the age of the person who is baptized (infant or adult) and of the particular theology of the church that sponsors the baptism, at some point in the process of "joining the church" an assent to a creedal statement or an affirmation of belief in Jesus as the Christ is made. For the person who is baptized as an infant, and therefore incapable of professing a belief in Jesus at the precise moment of baptism, the gathered community of faith in general and the parents in particular respond for the child. Later in life, the person will participate in some form of Confirmation service at which time the individual will make a public confession of faith. For the person who is baptized as an adult, the profession

of faith in Jesus is usually made just prior to the moment of baptism. Therefore, "belief" plays an active role in the Christian rite of initiation into the church.

2. As recorded in Exodus 6:6: "Say therefore to the people of Israel, 'I am the Lord, and I will bring you out from under the burdens of the Egyptians, and I will deliver you from their bondage, and I will redeem you with an outstretched arm and with great acts of judgment . . .'" (RSV).

3. As recorded in Genesis 12:3: "I will bless those who bless you, and him who curses you I will curse; and by you all the families of the earth will bless themselves" (RSV).

Chapter Three

Differences Between Judaism and Christianity

We have already identified some of the significant differences between Christianity and Judaism—in their specific Structures and in how the Individual adherent progresses through it to his Religion. We have also cited a difference in the intent of the worship services. We now turn our attention to a number of other familiar, though frequently unrecognized or misunderstood, differences that we find between the two Religions. Although some of these variations are often taken for granted, they can be more clearly appreciated as appropriate for each Religion when viewed through this Structural approach.

CHRISTIAN MANIFESTATIONS

We start with a number of Christian examples. As we have already indicated, if one wishes to be recognized and accepted by other Christians as a Christian, participation in a specific church is mandated. According to the Structure, the denominations and their churches are the Rays of Christianity. They are what give substance and meaning to the Individual who calls himself a Christian. By joining a church in one's community and becoming active in it, the Individual gives evidence that he believes in Christ and is willing to attest to this belief via membership and participation in an organized community of faith. Ideally this affiliation will be more than perfunctory (with the person's name merely included on the church rolls), but it will be more substantive and will include an active involvement in many of the church's activities on a regular and on-going basis. Without some sort of church membership, at the very least, the person's status as a Christian will be questioned by other Christians.

The fact that the Rays of the Structure stand for the various churches of Christendom reveals an interesting, yet familiar, phenomenon in American Christian life known as "church hopping." Such behavior is the bane of denominational leadership because it undermines denominational loyalty. In our mobile society families often move from community to community, and when they do, they frequently do not affiliate with a church in their new community that is a member of the same denomination as the one to which they belonged in their prior place of residence. Thus we might find a family moving every few years, and in so doing becoming in succession a member of a Baptist church because their neighbors belong, then a Methodist church because of its fine youth program for their children, and finally a Presbyterian church because they are fond of the minister and admire his sermons. Or, church-hopping may occur as a result of marriage. President George W. Bush is an example of this kind of phenomenon. He was brought up as both an Episcopalian and a Presbyterian, but became a Methodist after his marriage to his wife, Laura, as that was her Protestant affiliation. This pattern of "church hopping" does not disturb the family's Faith-Belief in Christ, the Bridge-Link to the Essential Element of the Structure. The shift occurs among the Rays of Christianity.

Another manifestation of the Christian Structure occurs with particular religious symbols. Perhaps the most obvious public symbol is the crèche, the nativity scene, often placed in front of a church at Christmas time. Its message incorporates Faith-Belief in Christ but not in a specific denomination or church. That is, there are no Catholic or Protestant crèches. Crèches are Christian by nature but not denominationally specific.

The most frequently seen personal Christian symbol is a cross, usually worn on a chain about the neck. This jewelry is intended to send a message to those who see it of the wearer's Faith-Belief in Christ. Note though that there is no way of telling to which denomination the cross wearer belongs, unless that cross is specifically a Roman Catholic one with Jesus on it, or similarly if the jewelry is a Miraculous Medal or a pendant with Mary on it. In a similar way, the bracelet with the letters "WWJD" (What Would Jesus Do?) indicates the wearer's belief without being denominationally specific.

Another symbol that one sees, though with less frequency, is found on the back of automobiles, a fish with the word "Jesus" in it. Here, too, is an affirmation of Faith-Belief in Christ that the owner of the car wishes to advertise, but again it does not automatically indicate a particular denomination. And there are people in some parts of the country who erect three crosses on their property that are visible from the highway, with the middle one taller than the other two, symbolic of the crucifixion narrative. Again, this configuration represents a statement of Faith-Belief. However, none of these symbols in-

volves the Rays of Christianity. They are all generically Christian and therefore reflect a generalized Faith-Belief in Christ.

Christian revivals and "spiritual renewals" can also be better understood
when they are viewed through the perspective of the Structure. Both of these
activities focus on Faith-Belief in Christ, though each has a slightly different
purpose. The revival is usually intended to bring the non-churched person to
Christ, while the spiritual renewal program tends to focus on strengthening
the Faith-Belief component of the already churched Christian. Both activities
initially address the Faith-Belief element of the Structure and then expect an
increased level of participation in a church—either a new church for the person declaring his acceptance of Christ as his personal savior at the revival, or
the church of which he is already a member for the participant in a spiritual
renewal program. Regardless, the desired outcome of both activities is the
same. They focus on implementing an involvement in the Christian Rays after the person's Religion is affirmed.

Christian worship can also be better understood through the Structure. The
sermon or homily frequently focuses the congregation's attention on some
aspect of Christ's life, with the intent of strengthening Faith-Belief in Him.
Many churches advertise themselves as "Christ Centered," echoing the Essential Element of Christ in Christianity. When the congregation sings
hymns, the words of these songs frequently proclaim the message of Faith-
Belief. And Christian prayers, as we indicated earlier, more often than not,
conclude with such words as "In the name of the Father, Son and Holy
Spirit," "In Christ's name we pray," or some other phrase that expresses the
Faith-Belief of the person offering the prayer, as well as that of the congregation assembled.

Traditional Christian theology also reflects this Structure. It is a product
of the need to define Christian Faith-Belief. The Bridge-Link needs elabora-
tion so that the "faithful" will know in what they need to have faith and the
"believer" will know what to believe. In order to achieve this goal, Christianity at a very early stage developed creeds, each one more refined than the
previous in detailing the nature and substance of orthodox Christian belief.
These creeds subsequently became a test of one's membership in the church
and even today they are recited by congregants in some liturgical worship
services.

However, creeds are rather straightforward statements, and they proved inadequate for the development of the nuances of Christian thought. As a result,
Christianity developed a large body of theological literature, most of which
attempted to present Christian thought and belief in an organized, systematic
fashion for those Christians (usually church scholars) who wanted to go beyond the creeds in their understanding of their religion. Both the creeds and

the theological tomes (often called dogmatic or systematic theology) had to be presented in an orderly and defining fashion so that "Faith-Belief" would be cogent, consistent, and coherent to believers.

All of these manifestations, and others which we shall consider in subsequent chapters, are the product of the Christian Structure. They make sense for the Christian, but they can be confusing to the Jew or non-religious person who encounters them without the benefit of knowing how they function in the Christian Structure. However, because Christianity is so pervasive in this country, these manifestations are generally taken for granted by most people.

JEWISH MANIFESTATIONS

Conversely, there are many manifestations that are the product of the Jewish Structure and which can be very confusing to Christians who do not know much about Judaism. More often than not, this confusion occurs because there are no counterparts within their own religion on which to base their understanding.

But before considering the Jewish manifestations that have no Christian counterparts, we need to look at one phenomenon that does have a peculiarly Jewish similarity. We began the discussion of Christian manifestations in this chapter with a description of "church hopping." This sort of occurrence also happens in Judaism, but it fits the Jewish Structure. One can find Jews who, when they move from community to community, were previously affiliated with a Conservative synagogue and subsequently join a Reform congregation in their new community, or vice versa. Both movements are part of the Jewish People and, for the Jew who affiliates with them in succession, worship patterns and specific outlooks between them are of lesser importance than their being Jewish places of worship. Or, we may find a family that has lived in a community for a number of generations, and who will belong and pay dues to an Orthodox synagogue because of family sentiment but who will attend and be active in a Reform or Conservative synagogue because they feel more comfortable there. Though they are supporting synagogues with divergent views of Jewish tradition, they feel no conflict because both kinds of synagogues are part of the Jewish people which, in their view, takes precedence.

We find an equally interesting difference between the two religions when we view what is considered religious art. Before the Renaissance, much of the Christian religious art which depicted people, centered on the events in Christ's life or the lives of the many saints which historic Christianity had canonized. There were also Biblical scenes that were depicted in elaborate church stained glass windows (and served as "text" for the illiterate). These presentations of people in Christian art were very much focused on Christ and events within church history.

By contrast, Jewish art, generally until modern times, did not depict people. The Biblical Second Commandment[1]was believed to have brought this about, although there are examples of Jewish art depicting human beings that counter this view and that were found in a few ancient synagogues. Nonetheless, throughout the ages Jewish art tended to be of a ceremonial nature, used in the celebration of Jewish holidays—an elaborately decorated menorah for Hanukkah, the Seder plate for Passover, special candles for the Sabbath. Interestingly, we also find medieval Haggadahs for the Passover Seder and scrolls of the Book of Esther for reading at Purim that may contain pictures of human beings. However, these books were also intended for children who could not read. It is only in modern times that Jewish pictorial art has begun to flourish. Some of this art is mystical, such as the works of Marc Chagall; much of it depicts Jewish ceremonial occasions—weddings, bar and bat mitzvahs. There is no depiction of God or of scenes that convey a theological message. The focus is very different, reflecting the difference in the Structure between the two religions.

We now move into the more obvious differences. Perhaps one of the most confusing phenomenons in Judaism for Christians today is the large number of "secular Jews." These are Jews who openly affirm that they are Jewish, are accepted as Jews by their fellow Jews, and are even seen as Jews by their gentile friends. On the one hand, they religiously never set foot in a synagogue, unless for obligatory family occasions. They want no part of what is commonly called religion or worship. They may question the existence of God, and may even profess atheism. On the other hand, they may be active in any number of non-synagogually affiliated Jewish organizations or activities, e.g., B'nai B'rith, Jewish War Veterans, Hadassah, etc. A Jew does not have to be a member of a synagogue to participate in these various organizations. In part this reflects the fact that most Jews are born Jewish, traditionally of a Jewish mother, and as a result there is no theological test for their being part of their religion. Furthermore, because these organizations are not synagogually based, their activities are not what might ordinarily be considered "religious" in the Christian understanding of the word. Nonetheless, they are one of the Rays of Judaism, one of the options for the person who declares himself or herself to be part of the historic Jewish People, but not "religious" in the usual sense of the word. Only a religion that does not require an affirmation of a Faith-Belief as the Bridge-Link of its Structure can function in this way.

An additional facet of secular Judaism in America is the existence of approximately 40 Humanist synagogues. Rabbi Sherwin Wine, the founder of this movement, is quoted in an article in the *Jewish Post and Opinion* of

February 20, 2002, that Humanist Judaism is intended for those Jews whose "faith has long since vanished," but whose "attachment to their (Jewish) roots remains strong." And Rabbi Adam Chalom, in the same issue of the *Jewish Post and Opinion* states that Humanist Judaism "is an important component of the Jewish community for those who are committed to pluralistic Judaism as a way to strengthen the community overall." He further describes it "as a combination of Jewish identity and community service" for those Jews who identify strongly as Jews but who do not believe in God. Again, only a religion that does not require a theological affirmation could have such a manifestation.

Similar to the phenomenon of Humanist Judaism are the people about whom Klein and Vuijust write in their book, *The Half-Jewish Book*. Some of these people, who have one Jewish parent, have chosen to be Jewish by acknowledging and participating in Jewish organizations. Others have chosen not to affiliate with Judaism but attend a church. This latter group of individuals, as seen through the Structure, should be labeled Christian because of their religious involvement. One would certainly not label them "half-Christians" if one of their parents was Christian and they identified themselves as Jewish. Yet the authors label the people about whom they write as "Half-Jews" primarily because they are using the Christian understanding of what the word "Religion" means and not a Jewish understanding. Thus their efforts only add to the confusion which this book is attempting to clarify.

In this same vein, the cover of Michelle Guinness' book, to which we referred earlier in chapter one, pictures the author on the cover wearing the six pointed Star of David, a Jewish symbol. She is a Christian, married to an Anglican minister. According to the Structure, such a symbol is no longer hers. She should be shown wearing a cross.

We previously mentioned some Christian symbols like the cross and the crèche. Judaism has symbols also, and the six pointed Star of David, that we just described Michelle Guinness as wearing, is one of them. Jewish chaplains in the military wear a seven branch candlestick, known as a menorah, as an insignia on their uniforms. Many Jewish people wear *Chai's*, the Hebrew letters *Het* and *Yod* meaning Life, as jewelry. These symbols speak more to the identity of the wearer than any specific aspect of his or her faith. On the other hand, the *Mezzuzah*, containing passages from the Torah is traditionally found on the doorpost of a Jewish home, Jewish art pieces used for Holiday observance—an artistic Kiddush cup for saying the blessing over the wine on the Sabbath or holidays, the Seder plate for Passover, and the eight branched menorah for Hanukkah—all have special religious meaning, but they make an identity statement as well. They are as apt to be found in the home of a ritually observant Jew as in the home of a Jew who seldom, if ever, attends the synagogue. Thus the message of Jewish symbols is not the same as those made by Christian symbols. They tend to bespeak identity, and not belief. An additional, and rather extreme, example of the use of Jewish symbols was a pair of socks on sale for Hanukkah that had six pointed stars and *dreydels* (Hanukkah tops) knitted into their design. It is hard to imagine someone selling socks with crosses in their pattern. That is not how one expresses his Faith-Belief.

Another manifestation of Judaism that very often confuses the Christian is the State of Israel as a religious concern for the Jew. As we indicated in our description of the Bridge-Link in relation to the Essential Element in Judaism, the Jew consciously identifies himself or herself as a part of the historic Jewish People. A People can return to the area of its geographic origins and, when they do, set up a political state. This occurred in the time of Ezra (fifth century B.C.E.) in the Bible. It also occurred in 1948, with the establishment of the modern State of Israel. Because of the Jewish understanding of what Religion encompasses, as well as the nature of the Jewish Structure, the modern Jew living outside of Israel is able to relate to what occurs there in the first person. It is a part of what a Jew understands as his or her Religion.

As illustration, the Jew who travels to Israel and views its antiquities is apt to respond, "This is where *my* ancestors did . . . ." And to the modern things in Israel, he is apt to say, "Look what *we* have done here." Both reactions involve the use of the first person pronoun. By contrast, when a Christian goes to the same bit of geography (which is often called the Holy Land rather than Israel), that person usually goes there to see where Christ did whatever he did at that ancient site, and to the modern things he is apt to respond, "Look what *they* have done here." The use of the different *personal* pronoun is telling. To the Jew, this geography and this State are a part of who he is as a Jew; to the Christian the antiquities he wants to see relate to Christ and the modern things pertain to citizens of another country with whom he feels no personal connection or identity.

Since there is no Christian "people" in the same way that we speak of the Jewish People, the State of Israel can be a very mystifying "religious" manifestation for the Christian. We shall spend a subsequent chapter illustrating how this difference became a major impasse to inter-religious dialogue as a result of the Six Day War in 1967. There has been no better illustration since then, nor one that is so well documented, of this stumbling block brought about by the structural difference between Christianity and Judaism.

Another difference between the two religions is that Judaism has languages. The Jewish Bible was originally written in Hebrew, the language that the ancient Israelites spoke every day. Over the centuries this language ceased being a spoken language but remained the language of Jews for both study and worship. A good deal of post-Biblical Jewish literature is in Hebrew, though not necessarily Biblical Hebrew. And with the settlement of Palestine by Jewish immigration in the early part of the twentieth century, Hebrew was resurrected and once more became a spoken, living language as it is today in the State of Israel (though with many modern words having to be devised and added to the vocabulary to make it current). It is difficult to really understand Jewish religious literature, whether the Bible or post-Biblical literature, without an understanding of the nuances contained in the Hebrew text. This is similarly the case with the prayer book, though many of the prayers are translated, or even paraphrased, into English. But the original Hebrew meaning of the words often does not translate very well and may encompass far more than the meaning of the English equivalent.

From the time of the Middle Ages, there were two other major Jewish languages, both of which have come down to us today. One is Yiddish, spoken in Central and Eastern Europe by the Jews of that area. This language is a patois which had its origins in medieval German with the addition of Hebrew, Slavic, and other Eastern European languages of the areas in which Jews lived. It is written in Hebrew characters and thus reads from right to left as Hebrew does. The other language, usually identified as Ladino, is spoken by the Jews from the Mediterranean basin and is a medieval Spanish with the addition of Hebrew, Arabic, and other languages of that area, and is also written in Hebrew characters. Although many of those who spoke these languages lost their lives during the Holocaust, there are still many Jews alive today who continue to speak them. And there is also a good deal of literature and music in both of these languages.

In addition to these three major Jewish languages, many of the Jewish communities scattered about the world also developed their own languages, though most of them have disappeared with the disappearance of these communities in modern times.

By comparison, Christianity knows no indigenous languages. In Christendom, languages are the manifestation of geography or of national groups, i.e., French, Italian, English, etc. Even the Roman Catholic Church was able to cease using Latin in its liturgy, since it was not a language integral to the Bridge Link or Essential Element. While it was taken over from the Roman Empire and used for centuries in both worship and study, Latin is not inherently a "Christian" language. Because a people can have languages, Judaism has languages. Because there are no Christian "people" per se, Christianity does not have any indigenous religious languages.

We find a similar difference in manifestation between the two religions in the area of foods and food ways. One can find any number of excellent Jewish cookbooks on the shelves of book stores. Many of them reflect the traditions of the Jews of Eastern Europe, but there are also Jewish cookbooks from Israel, and from many of the other Jewish communities scattered about the world. Food ways are the manifestation of a group of people, here the Jewish People. They are also the product of Jewish dietary laws, which adapted the foods of the areas of Jewish settlement to the requirements of these regulations. These two factors identify another Ray within Judaism that has no Christian counterpart, where food ways, like language, are a product of geography or national groups, i.e., French cooking, Italian cooking, English cooking, etc. There is no "Christian" cooking per se. The closest one can get are the many cookbooks compiled and published by individual churches, but these are hardly comparable. Although they contain the favorite recipes of those who have contributed to the cookbooks, they can hardly be labeled as "Christian" cookbooks. Here then is another Jewish Ray that can be a source of confusion in inter-religious discussion, but which makes sense when viewed through the Structure.

Yet another difference is found in Jewish humor. Again, we can find many anthologies of Jewish humor in a good book store. This humor reflects the experiences of the Jewish People, often with stories that are self-deprecating, a laughing at oneself and the predicament in which one finds oneself as a Jew. Much of this humor came about as a way of dealing with the persecution and suppression found in an anti-Jewish world. By laughing at the situation, the Jew was better able to survive difficulties. Even this humor was a way of telling the oppressor that there was little that could be done to the Jew that had not already happened and which he had survived. Jewish humor touches upon every facet of life, bringing a bit of irony or cynicism to a situation, trying to overcome the difficulties that life presents by seeing its humorous side. By contrast, Christianity really does not have such humor. The best one can find is an off-color story about a priest or a nun, or perhaps a Protestant minister caught in an embarrassing situation with a congregant. In Christendom once more, humor is a national or geographic phenomenon. It is not a Ray, as it is in Judaism.

Differences in religious music are not as confusing in inter-religious discussion as are the above examples. There is church music, and it has its counterpart in synagogue music. There is also some non-church Christian music, modern rock music that, as one might expect, reflects a Faith-Belief in Christ. Judaism also has non-synagogual music. We can find modern rock music here as well. However, it usually is not about Faith-Belief, but rather picks up on some theme found within Jewish tradition, perhaps a Biblical verse or even a rabbinic text. In addition, there is also a great deal of other music that is labeled as Jewish—Yiddish lullabies, Ladino love songs, modern Israeli folk tunes. The scope of what is considered to be Jewish music is much broader than that which is considered Christian music, again reflecting the difference between a religion based on a statement of belief over against a religion coming from a group of people. The differences here are not as obvious as some of the ones considered previously, but they are present and can bring about problems in inter-religious understanding.

We have already spoken about Christian theology. The Jewish counterpart is better labeled "religious ideas," since "theology" (the study of God) is not identical within Judaism, even though some Jewish thinkers have used this word because many of the areas of concern are similar. As we indicated earlier, Christian theology tends to be orderly and systematic, defining beliefs so that the Christian can know what his faith encompasses. In sharp contrast, Jewish religious ideas are non-systematic and non-definitive. They tend to be situational or dialogical. If an idea is appropriate for one situation it is used, but if it is inappropriate for another, then it is laid aside (not negated) for possible use in yet another situation where it will once more be appropriate. In addition, Jewish religious ideas are not presented in a systematic fashion. Rather, they tend to be more stream of consciousness in style, that is, one idea leading into the next, and then into the next, or they may be anecdotal stories or even parables used as illustration. Orderliness is not necessary since it is not what one believes (the Bridge-Link in Christianity) that brings one in or keeps one out of Judaism. In this regard, Marie Noonan Sabin, a Roman Catholic educator, in her book, *Reopening the Word*, which is a study of the Jewish background of the Gospel of Mark, comments that "when one explores any body of writings in Early Judaism, what one finds is not logical, organized theology but multiple, shifting images that convey different angles of truth."[2] She further states that historic Jewish religious thought "perceives God's word to be a dynamic, unending source of new disclosures, a timeless word that is relevant to changing times, an open-ended, on going revelation."[3]

This approach is still very much present today. Judaism's Bridge-Link, as we have seen, is one's Conscious Self-Identification. As a result, Christian Faith-Belief and Jewish Religious Ideas occur in different locations within their separate Structures, the former being the Bridge-Link and the latter being a Ray. Consequently, they function differently because they play a very different role within each religion. The best illustration of this difference was the "Death of God" controversy in the late 1960s and early 1970s. Although this event occurred three decades ago, there has not been such a good illustration of this difference since that time. We shall devote most of a subsequent chapter to this interesting phenomenon.

Our examination of these differences between Judaism and Christianity has illustrated the value of the Structure of Religion to better overcome many of the misunderstandings that occur between Judaism and Christianity. Although some of these are quite familiar to the reader, they are often confusing or overlooked. When framed by their respective Structure, however, these differences can be seen as both intelligible and appropriate.

NOTES

1. "You shall not make for yourself a graven image, or any likeness of anything that is in heaven above, or that is in the earth beneath, or that is in the water under the earth . . ." (Exodus 20:4, RSV).

2. Marie Noonan Sabin, *Reopening the Word* (Oxford: Oxford University Press, 2002), 157.

3. Ibid., 202.

Chapter Four

Conversion

Now that we have described the Structure and some resulting differences between the two religions, we need to examine in detail how one converts to either Judaism or Christianity. Although conversions in and out of both Religions occur in accordance with the general Structure, in specifics, they vary tremendously. We will also want to consider why Christianity is evangelical by nature, while Judaism is not. Both of these dynamics influence each religion's views about conversion.

CONVERSION TO CHRISTIANITY

Again we start with Christianity because that is what is probably more familiar to the reader. By using the Structure as our guide, we see that the person who converts to Christianity must come to believe in Christ, i.e., the Individual must espouse a personal Faith-Belief in Christ (God). Whether through an emotional conversion experience as found in more conservative denominations, or through an intellectual process that convinces the person of the reality of the Christian message as found in more liberal denominations, the Individual must make a declaration of Faith-Belief (the Bridge-Link) in the Essential Element—Christ (God)—in order to enter Christianity. Once he concludes this personal journey, the convert needs to join a church (a Ray) in order to complete the conversion process. Throughout the centuries both the Christian tradition and local congregations have provided rituals of initiation (usually Baptism) by which the person becomes formally received into the community of faith.

The opposite occurs when a person intentionally disassociates himself from Christianity, and becomes an apostate. The individual in some meaningful and obvious way may deny his or her Faith-Belief in Christ (though not necessarily in God) and leave the church (assuming the person had been a member). He no longer accepts Christianity as his Religion. Such a person may do this by no longer attending a church and may even tell those whom he knows and loves that this is his decision and what he is doing; less obviously he may just do this quietly without informing anyone of what he has decided. Regardless of which route he chooses, internally he has made the decision to cease being a Christian and, more often than not, enters into what might be called "religious limbo," with no obvious religious affiliation.

Within the traditional Christian frame of reference, the person who publicly ceases to be a Christian may cause some concern among his Christian family and friends. The cause of this reaction often emanates from the historic reason for becoming a Christian in the first place—salvation. Throughout the centuries, the church, with its evangelical, conversionist message proclaimed that the non-Christian should convert to Christianity in order to be "saved." Because salvation is part of God's divine plan (or providence), conversion secures eternal life for the individual after death. Accordingly, the non-Christian would not be blessed with this reward in the hereafter. Even today the traditional Christian is still apt to maintain this basic reason for believing in Christ. Consequently, when someone a Christian knows or loves denies this belief, in essence, that person is declaring that he is willing to forfeit his place in heaven. The willingness of the apostate to forsake this opportunity can be both confounding and upsetting to the person who seriously embraces this Christian axiom. And not only can it be distressing, it can also be very threatening to the believer, because the apostate has raised a fundamental question about the essential truth of Christianity: Can a Christian admit the validity of Judaism or any other religion without compromising belief in the uniqueness and the finality of Jesus as the Christ? What if the apostate is correct? It then follows that the person who retains his Christian belief is wrong. Thus, the departure of one Christian from the community of faith can threaten the whole Structure of Christianity for the believer. The Faith-Belief Bridge-Link of Christianity is both foundational and fragile. Therefore, as we shall later discuss in chapter six with the "Death of God" theology, any obvious challenge to the Bridge-Link component of the Christian Structure, specifically the Faith-Belief brought about by apostasy, may elicit a highly emotional response within the committed Christian.

As part of our consideration of the process of conversion to Christianity, we also need to examine the traditional Christian emphasis on evangelism— the active process of seeking converts, something that Judaism has not done for millennia.[1] One needs to ask, what accounts for this difference in behavior and attitude between the two religions? A frequent reason cited by Christians to justify evangelism is the Biblical injunction in Jesus' words to "make disciples of all nations" (Matthew 28:19). Most Christians take this statement as a mandate to actively seek converts.

However, when we analyze the Christian propensity to conversion *via the Structure*, we glean two additional and startling insights. Momentarily we need to suspend our discussion of Religion, and place our inquiry within the framework of an argument. When two people argue, either one of them can come away from that argument with one of two polar possibilities. First, the other party is totally wrong and therefore put that person down by denying whatever he says. Second, one party can become open to the views of the other party, rethink his own position, subsequently accept his opponent's argument and abandon his prior position. When we examine this possible scenario from the perspective of the Structure, we see that historically the Christian could not take the second possibility. That alternative challenges and can even undermine his Faith-Belief in Christ.

For the second insight into evangelism, we need to move once more out of a religious frame of reference and take our example from the realm of sports. When we ask in this context, "What is the best defense?" we usually get the reply, "Why, a good offense, of course." When we take that response and place it back into the structural Faith-Belief of the Christian Bridge-Link, we discover that the conversionist approach of Christianity thwarts the possible erosion of Faith-Belief. By actively seeking and winning converts to Christ, an offensive strategy, there is no reason for the Christian to reconsider and question his acceptance of the Christian theological message. Moreover, the convert confirms the truth of the Christian Faith-Belief for the converter. Conversely, however, the failure of evangelism to convince a prospective convert could initiate a series of self-doubts for the Christian missionary. Hence, evangelism, viewed from the vantage point of the Structure, acts as a defensive mechanism for Christianity.[2]

In essence, our Structure informs us that the successful process of evangelizing individuals to Christianity strengthens the Faith-Belief element of the already committed Christian, while the unsuccessful process, either by an apostate's departure from the fold or by a person's refusal to convert in the face of Christian evidence, undermines the Christian Faith-Belief component. Hence, Faith-Belief, the Bridge-Link of Christianity, the element that initiates the process of making a person a Christian, is the most emotionally laden part of the Structure.

CONVERSION TO JUDAISM

We now turn our attention to the process of conversion to Judaism. From the standpoint of the general Structure, the process is identical to what we found in Christianity. The Individual through the Bridge-Link to the Jewish People comes into his or her new Religion. This Bridge-Link as we saw earlier is one's Conscious Self-Identification. Consequently, the person who was not born a Jew and wishes to convert must build this Identification within himself in order to change the response to the word "Jew" from the second or third person to that of the first person. When this occurs, the convert identifies with the historic Jewish People, in the same way that the person born into a Jewish family does through his upbringing. For the convert, this process most often involves a lengthy period of study, as well as participation in Jewish activities (Rays), usually beginning with but not limited to the synagogue, the Jewish counterpart to the church in Christianity. In addition, the identity formation may also involve a trip to Israel, the observance of Jewish rituals and festivals in the home, and learning Hebrew. As we saw from the Rays in the Jewish Structure, there are many manifestations of Judaism, and the person wanting to become a Jew can involve himself in any of them.

As in Christianity, there is a ritual which signifies the completion of the conversion journey. For a male, it may involve ritual circumcision, which for an adult may be the full operation if he is uncircumcised, or merely the taking of a drop of blood if he is circumcised. For both men and women, the process also includes appearing before a *Bet Din*, a court of three rabbis, who usually question the convert's motives for conversion, as well as ask the person specific questions about Judaism to determine whether he has grasped the rudiments of his new Religion. There may follow a trip to the *Mikveh*, a ritual bath, in which the convert immerses himself or herself, and recites a number of blessings which signify his or her conversion. There may also be an additional ceremony in the synagogue. As part of this process, the convert also receives a Jewish name, often one that he or she has selected, followed by *ben* or *bat Avraham v'Sarah*, (the child of Abraham and Sarah). This new name links the convert, as a Jew, all the way back to Abraham and Sarah — the Biblical ancestors of all Jews as recorded in the Book of Genesis. According to rabbinic tradition, once a person converts to Judaism, there is to be no mention of the individual's prior religion. The convert is now a Jew just like anyone who is born a Jew. There is no "former" Christian, a word used with some Jews who convert to Christianity.

In the same way that we considered the Christian reaction to the Christian apostate, we also need to explore the Jewish reaction to the Jewish apostate. Again, the structural process is identical but the specifics vary between the two Religions. Like Christianity, the process of getting out of Judaism is just the opposite of getting in. The Individual ceases to identify himself as being a part of the historic people; he denies the Bridge-Link for himself. He may do this in an obvious fashion by converting to another religion, most commonly in the United States to Christianity. Or, he may withdraw from the Jewish community through non-participation and become assimilated into the general population. Or, he may marry a non-Jew and raise his children as non-Jews, with the process thus taking another generation or maybe two, to complete, as with many "half-Jews." Thus, there can be both active and passive apostates.

The traditional Jewish reaction to the apostate, or even the person marrying a non-Jew, as one might suspect, is quite negative. In the Passover Seder, the ritual meal associated with that holiday, it is the *Wicked Son* who asks, "What mean '*You*' (plural) by this ceremony?" And the answer to him is that because he says "*You*" and not "*We*," he would not have been worthy of participating in the exodus from Egypt which culminated in the theophany at Mount Sinai. As previously mentioned, the son uses the wrong pronoun and thereby removes himself from being a part of the Jewish People. Hence, the son earned the title, "Wicked Son." The traditional family reaction, therefore, to both the apostate and the person marrying a non-Jew, was to sit *shiva*, the seven-day ritual of mourning. That person was considered dead. By intentionally denying any participation in the Covenant that God made with the Jewish People at Mount Sinai (the Relationship of the People to God), that individual became a "traitor" and was never mentioned by the family again. Among less traditional Jews today this extreme reaction is not apt to occur. Nonetheless, even non-observant, non-practicing Jews may express some concern about Jewish continuity within their family when they are faced with the possibility of non-Jewish grandchildren.

Now that we understand the Jewish Structure, it is easy to see why the subject of mixed marriage (between a Jew and a non-Jew) holds a very prominent position on the American Jewish agenda. There have been numerous studies made on this subject, most of them decrying the increased rate of marriage between Jews and persons not born Jewish. Rabbi Adam Fisher, in a paper on the subject in *The CCAR Journal* (Spring, 1973), brings this concern to a very personal level when he observes that such a marriage is "painful to Jewish parents because their hopes for the continuity of Jewish life in their own families have been shattered." This need for "continuity" reflects the unique Jewish Structure and has no equivalent structural element in Christianity.

The need for continuity introduces us to a relatively new and modern phenomenon, the Jew who converts to Christianity but finds it difficult to give up his or her Jewish Identity. This person, while professing a belief in Jesus (usually referred to as *Yeshua*) and thereby becoming Christian, wishes at the same time to remain a part of the Jewish People. (This situation is modern because most converts to Christianity in earlier times wanted to forget that they had been Jews.) These people refer to themselves by such names as "Jews for Jesus," "Messianic Jews," or even "Completed Jews." They accept the Christian belief in the messiahship of Christ, a message central to Christianity as we have already seen, and yet at the same time they wish to present themselves as Jews, attempting to blend the two religions as if they were not two distinct historic traditions. These individuals fail to comprehend the Structure as we have delineated it. Judaism represents the continuity of an historic group of people, while Christianity emphasizes the Faith-Belief of the individual. In their religious life these Jewish converts to Christianity openly affirm the latter religion, but fail to realize that by so doing, they have removed themselves from the Jewish People. Although they deny our interpretation, Judaism does not affirm a Faith-Belief system. Moreover, they fail to understand that for their children and grandchildren, Judaism will become only a family memory, a point which Klein and Vuijst, as well as Michelle Guinness, seem to overlook. The Jewish Rays will have no place in their daily religious life. Faith-Belief in Christ, the Christian Structure, will be their *modus operandi*. The early Christians knew this when they separated themselves from Pharisaic Judaism by forgoing circumcision and the dietary laws (see Acts 15 and Galatians 2).

Rabbi Carol Harris-Shapiro, in her fine book *Messianic Judaism*,[3] has conducted an in-depth study of the attitudes and self-perceptions of many Messianic Jews who are members of B'nai Mashiah synagogue in fictional "Liberty City." She describes at length their desire for "salvation" in the Christian usage of the word and how this emphasis permeates their lives as Messianic Jews. They desire both to believe in Jesus and to be considered a part of the Jewish People. It does not work! For our purposes, in relating "Jews for Jesus" to the Structure, the author's comments about successive generations is most instructive: "As the second generation grows to teenager and adulthood, having no knowledge of Judaism besides what takes place in Messianic synagogues, there is also a danger of this generation losing the sentimental attachment to songs and prayers that the first generation took for granted." The second generation will move into the Christian Structure because that is where they feel most at home. In a similar fashion, many of the children of the "Half-Jews" discussed in the Klein and Vujist book follow the same pattern. The Judaism of one set of grandparents will become a family memory. Succeeding generations will not have any continued awareness of the family having been a Jewish family, a part of the Jewish People.

There is still another possibility when a person leaves Judaism. We refer here to that individual who wishes to remain "religious," but who does not wish to stay Jewish or affirm a Faith-Belief in the traditional Trinitarian view of Christ (God). Within recent times this person would most likely join the

Unitarian/Universalist Church. Unfortunately, this move is also problematic. The Structure informs us that theology, which forms the basis for Faith-Belief and is central to Christianity, is not essential to Judaism. It occurs as Religious Ideas in the Rays. They are not structurally equal. Furthermore, while Unitarianism denies the Trinity, it does not affirm any affiliation with the Jewish People. Thus the Jew who becomes a Unitarian/Universalist is really an apostate. He is not exchanging his prior Religion for one that functions in the same way, but rather for one that functions more as a Christian denomination (since many Unitarian/Universalist members have previously been affiliated with some form of Trinitarian Christianity).

Earlier in this chapter we mentioned that Judaism has not been conversionist in the same way as Christianity. This distinction puzzles many people. If Jews believe that Judaism is the "true" religion, they too should actively seek new adherents. Again, the Jewish Structure provides insight. Jewish Faith-Belief occurs after one is already a Jew. It is not the Bridge-Link as is the case in Christianity. Thus the non-Jew, who does not convert to Judaism after learning about it, is not perceived as a threat as the non-believer is in Christianity. In Judaism, there is no need to defend Faith-Belief through active evangelism as we find in Christianity. The specific Structure of each Religion clearly explains this difference. And as we have previously mentioned, the Bridge-Link is the emotional element of each Structure. In Christianity, a threat to the Bridge-Link may well result in a passionately charged defense or even denial of that which appears to undermine the Christian Faith-Belief. In Judaism, a threat to the emotional Bridge-Link elicits a defensive reaction at the level of Conscious Self-Identification as a Jew. The Anti-Defamation League and numerous other "secular" Jewish organizations, which fight anti-Semitism both in the United States and abroad, represent a reaction within the Bridge-Link of Judaism. They often present emotional appeals for funds which frequently emphasize this ongoing threat. Christianity does not have a counterpart—a non-church related group that responds to anti-Christian activity throughout the world. This comparison underscores the value of the Structure to clarify these differences. Although each religion responds to threats to its Bridge-Link, each response is religion specific and appropriate as depicted by the Structure.

NOTES

1. In his article "Did Ancient Jews Missionize?" in *Bible Review* (August 2003), Shaye J. D. Cohen argues that with the single exception of the second century B.C.E. Maccabean period Judaism was never a missionary religion like Christianity. Al-

though the Jewish leaders during the time of Jesus and the rabbis up until the time that Constantine made Christianity the official religion of the Roman Empire in the fourth century, when conversion to Judaism became a capital crime, never sponsored organized missions to the gentiles, they generally exhibited an open attitude to outsiders and usually accepted gentile converts who expressed an interest in becoming Jewish. Cohen qualifies the historical importance of Matthew 23:15—the only ancient source that explicitly ascribes a missionary policy to a Jewish group—since its meaning is unclear (literal or metaphorical) and its value is uncertain (exception or norm).

2. This discussion does not attempt to present a comprehensive treatment of the motives and reasons for Christian proselytism through the centuries. Rather, it highlights the distinct perspective the Structure offers on the topic of Christian evangelism.

3. Carol Harris-Shapiro, *Messianic Judaism* (Boston: Beacon Press, 1999).

Chapter Five

The State of Israel

As we indicated in chapter three, the State of Israel, often referred to as the Holy Land by Christians, is a "religious" phenomenon for Jews. It has no counterpart within Christianity, since there is no (modern) "Christian" nation per se, not even the Vatican which is holy only to Roman Catholicism. Therefore the Jewish reaction to Israel can cause a great deal of confusion among Christians who want to understand how and why Jews relate to this modern political state as they do. Because it is *sui generis,* there are some Jews who also have difficulty understanding why so many other Jews vociferously and financially support this state. Furthermore, Jews need an interpretive structure by which they can explain to their Christian friends what it means to them.

The best illustration of the misunderstanding between Christians and Jews concerning the State of Israel occurred during the Six Day War in June of 1967. Although our example is dated, there has not been a better or more extensively documented case since that time. There are many books which have been written about the war, how it started and the events which took place both before and during it. For those who are interested in pursuing that topic more thoroughly, Michael B. Oren's book, *Six Days of War,*[1] has a lengthy and detailed bibliography of books and articles on the subject.

Because the purpose of this book is to provide a structural comparison between Judaism and Christianity, we are not going to consider the issues that brought about the War. We want to focus on the confused reactions to the War which happened in this country both during and after it. Moreover, this confusion did not occur only among Christians, but also among Jews, especially among some national rabbinic leaders who were trying so very hard to explain to their Christian counterparts the significance that the State of Israel and the War held for Jews. Many of these rabbis had been involved in inter-religious dialogues with nationally recognized Protestant and Catholic clergy for a number of years. They thought that the rapport established between them, as a result of the openness which they had worked so hard to forge, would sustain mutually beneficial and informative conversations about the War. However, everyone was surprised to realize how little fundamental understanding existed between the leadership of the two religions when this conflict began.

With the outbreak of the Six Day War in Israel in June 1967, both of these groups discovered to their dismay and confusion that what they had thought was a well-grounded dialogue between them was not that at all. As a matter of fact, the dialogues abruptly ceased with the outbreak of the War and did not resume until some six months later, even then in a halting form and with a very different agenda. The War was the catalyst for a whole new level of dialogue that has continued until this day. Yet, this shift was neither anticipated nor planned by the participants.

Prior to the Six Day War the agendas of these dialogues primarily focused on the two great social problems of the day, civil rights and poverty, and how the different religious communities could cooperatively respond. In these areas of concern, there was a great deal of mutual understanding and agreement. However, there was another level to the dialogues that transpired simultaneously. Honest attempts were made by each group to assist participants to better understand the differences in religious beliefs among them. It was this exact area of the dialogues that posed the problem during the Six Day War. As we have already learned, such discussions did not address equivalent parts of the two Structures. Matters of Faith-Belief comprise the Bridge-Link in Christianity, while matters of Faith-Belief are among the Rays in Judaism. They are not co-equal within the Structure of the two religions. The counterpart to the Christian Faith-Belief in Christ for Judaism is Conscious Self-Identification with the Jewish People. And just as anything that threatens Faith-Belief in Christianity (as we shall see subsequently in our consideration of the "Death of God" Theology in chapter six) can elicit a highly emotional reaction among Christians, so too does anything that threatens or, in this example, affects the Conscious Self-Identification of Jews within Judaism. And that is exactly what happened. Israel, with which American Jews consciously identify to varying degrees, was threatened militarily by her Arab neighbors. The War broke out and the American Jewish community reacted appropriately according to the Structure—it was happening to a part of *me* and *I* had better do something. However, since few, if any, of the rabbis or the Christian clergy at that time understood how the other's Structure functions, most of them reacted in confusion to the other, rather than with a clear grasp of the structural dynamics.

Before we treat the specifics of what happened as a result of the War, we need to present a brief review of how the State of Israel evolved. After the destruction of Jerusalem in 70 C.E. and the two unsuccessful Jewish revolts against Rome in the first and second centuries of the Common Era, the initial Jewish desire to return to Jerusalem (the city became symbolic of the whole geographic area) was a "religious" yearning expressed in prayer. For centuries, Jews have voiced this hope three times a day in worship. It is also recited at the conclusion of the Passover Seder and in the synagogue at the end of the solemn day of fasting on Yom Kippur. This yearning was connected to the Jewish hope for the coming of the Messiah, when all Jews, both living and dead, would return to the Holy City. Although the logistics of such a wonderful feat were God's concern, speculation about how and when all of this would happen was endless.

In the latter part of the nineteenth century, this ancient hope moved from the realm of prayer into the realm of politics. Modern nationalism was stirring in Eastern Europe among the Poles, Hungarians, and Romanians. They all wanted to establish their own independent states. The Jews living in these geographic areas also wished to join them in this effort. However, they were rejected. Because they were not considered Poles, or Hungarians, or Romanians, but Jews, they were not allowed to participate in these national efforts for independence. What heretofore they had thought was a "religion" (Judaism) was now being seen as a "nationality." And since they were perceived in political terms by their neighbors, they began to think of themselves in these terms, too. As a result, they started to ask a fundamental question about their own identity: If we are a nation, then where is our country and what is our language? Naturally they turned to the Bible and concluded that their land was the ancient land of the Children of Israel, then called Palestine, and their language, the ancient language of the Bible, Hebrew.

At the same time that this process unfolded in Eastern Europe, an assimilated Jewish newspaperman (not an observant Jew), Theodor Herzl, began asking similar questions about Jewish existence. In response to the anti-Semitic Dreyfus trial in France, in which Colonel Alfred Dreyfus was charged with treason on trumped up charges, Herzl wrote a book, published in 1896, entitled *The Jewish State*, in which he outlined the need for and the structure of an independent Jewish political state somewhere in the world. This book so galvanized the nascent Jewish nationalist movement in Eastern Europe that the following year the First Zionist Congress convened in Basle, Switzerland, to establish the international political Zionist movement. This marked the first step in a long and tortuous route, including the Holocaust, to the establishment of the State of Israel in May of 1948. It was to this ancient "homeland" that many of the survivors of the Nazi concentration camps went to begin new

lives of freedom in an independent Jewish State. Most American Jewry celebrated this unprecedented event by supporting their co-religionists in Israel
with financial aid, as well as visits to see how that country and their fellow
Jews were progressing. Although the welfare of Israel was high on the American Jewish agenda, uncertainty about the existence of the new nation
persisted. Some groups voiced concerns about the problems of "separation
of church and state" in Israel. Other groups worried about the possibility of
American Jews being labeled as disloyal to the United States. Israel was a
new experience for everyone and many people, both Jews and Christians, did
not know how to respond; nor did the American Jewish community realize
how emotionally involved it was in Israel's survival, or why.

With the outbreak of the Six Day War, Jews throughout the world rallied to
the defense of what they saw as a beleaguered Israel. They intuitively realized
that a part of them, the Jews of Israel, was being threatened by their surrounding Arab neighbors, and therefore they quickly responded in support of
the young nation. Our purpose, as we indicated earlier, is not to provide details about the War, but to focus on the reactions of American Christian clergy
and church organizations, as well as a number of prominent American rabbis,
to the War and to one another.

As soon as the War began, the rabbis involved in the national dialogues
called for the support of Israel by their Christian counterparts. The Jewish
People residing in Israel were under attack and this was a "religious" issue.
However, because the prior dialogues had never discussed Israel as a Jewish
religious concern, and because there is no parallel Christian nation in the
Christian Structure, these Christian leaders were unsure how to respond to
their rabbinic colleagues' requests for statements of concern for Israel. Many
remained silent. Furthermore, some of them expressed surprise at not only the
intensity of the rabbis' requests, but also the level of expectations the rabbis
had for church leaders. For Christians, the War was a political matter and not
a religious one. Father John B. Sheerin, a Paulist priest, wrote at that time,
"For most Christians the State of Israel seems to be . . . a political reality"
having no religious dimensions.

The Reverend William G. Oxtoby, writing in the July 26, 1967 issue of the
Christian Century, observed that, "The current crisis (in the dialogues caused
by the Six Day War) has revealed Jewish loyalties whose passionate intensity
few Christians had been aware of." And in an editorial in the August 1967 issue of the *Catholic World*, Father Sheerin again addressed this subject when
he wrote, "There are many Catholics . . . who had no realization whatsoever
that the survival of Israel had a profound significance for American Jews. It
took the grim reality of war as well as Arab threats to burst upon the American Jewish consciousness before we saw visible and tangible evidence of the

strong bond of kinship and interdependence uniting American and Israeli Jews."

What precipitated this realization within the Christian community was the vehement reaction of the Jewish community at the outbreak of the War. Individual Jews immediately responded in support of Israel. "*We* are being attacked and *we* have to do something," Jews everywhere were saying. They contributed large sums of money to help maintain the Israeli economy. Many young Jews dropped whatever they were doing and left for Israel to work in the fields and factories in place of those young Israelis who were called up to fight. American Jewish organizations hastily called public rallies in support of the Israeli cause and Jews spontaneously attended in large numbers. They firmly believed that the very existence of their fellow Jews in Israel was endangered and that another Holocaust was possible. Consequently, they were determined to prevent such a disaster from happening once more to a part of *us*.

When this short war concluded, Jews were not only jubilant that their worst fears had not been realized, but also proud. This increased sense of pride was reported in *The New York Times*, in an article on June 8, 1967, quoting a young Jew in that city as saying, "I really do feel prouder today. There is a new meaning to being Jewish."

When the War broke out, as we have indicated, the religious leaders of American Jewry turned to their Christian counterparts with whom they had been in dialogue for a number of years and asked for their support on both an individual and national level. As we have seen, these church leaders were unprepared for such a request. Rabbi David Polish wrote about this dialogical impasse in the July 26, 1967 issue of the *Christian Century*: "Clergymen and theologians were begged to sign statements of conscience in behalf of Israel, and in large numbers they refused." In the same issue of the magazine Reverend Oxtoby fittingly compared such a refusal "to a blasphemous attack on (Jewish) identity, almost as we (Christians) would regard an attack on Christ." (Note his unknowing use of the Structure). Unfortunately this comparison was not made in June, when most of the Christian leaders remained silent or else directed their appeals to a virtually immobilized United Nations, which stood by and did nothing.

Nonetheless, some Christian clergy did respond to the appeals for support made to them during the brief War. There was an advertisement in the June 4 issue of *The New York Times* signed by a number of prominent Christian clergy in support of the Israeli cause. And in Boston, His Eminence Richard Cardinal Cushing and a number of other Catholic and Protestant clergy signed an unambiguous "Declaration of Moral Principles" in support of Israel's position. On June 8 in Washington, D.C., Father Edward Flannery, a specialist in Catholic-Jewish relations, addressed a rally in support of Israel.

However these few, but outstanding leaders, were in the minority. A. Roy and Alice Eckhardt wrote in the July 26, 1967 issue of the *Christian Century* that "the few (Christian) voices that were raised merely helped to make the general stillness louder." Of the statements from many of the church leaders that did appear at the time, most were neutral or equivocal. The Eckhardts discovered that not one organized church body protested the Arab promise to annihilate Israel or supported Israel's right of self-defense. Because the Jewish Bridge-Link has no equivalent in the Christian Structure, most clergy were unsure how to respond. Their silence, however, spoke volumes about their inability to understand the significance of the War for their Jewish counterparts in particular and for the overall Jewish community in general.

As a result of the almost universal lack of support for the Israeli cause by the churches and their leaders, many of the rabbis who had participated in the Christian-Jewish dialogues over the years were upset. Most Jewish leaders had believed that these dialogues had established a good working relationship between them and their Christian colleagues. Therefore, they had expected that when an important part of the Jewish People was threatened, these same church leaders would understand the Jewish cries of anguish and speak out on behalf of Israel. However, the rabbis failed to realize that the dialogues had taken place without an awareness of the structural differences between the two religions. Their focus had been on social and moral issues, as well as theological differences; the role and place of the Jewish People was not on their agenda. Thus, the expectation that these church leaders would respond in support of Israel was ungrounded since the rabbis had not prepared them or themselves for this traumatic Jewish experience.

Because these rabbis did not know the Structure as we have presented it, they openly expressed anger and disappointment with their Christian colleagues. Instead of citing the inadequacies of the dialogues, they accused their colleagues of moral insensitivity. Rabbi Balfour Brickner, at the time the Director of the Commission on Inter-Faith (sic) Activities of the Union of American Hebrew Congregations, speaking before the Central Conference of American Rabbis in Los Angeles on June 22, 1967, said that the "organized church seemed unable to take a strong stand on what it considered to be a political issue," and concluded that "the survival of the Jewish People is not a political issue." Rabbi Marc Tannenbaum of the American Jewish Committee, addressing the annual meeting of the Religious Newsletters Association on July 7 of that year, criticized the "failure of the diplomatic institutions of Christendom to speak an unequivocal word in defense of the preservation of the Jewish People."

Shortly after the War many rabbis began to reconsider the failure of the dialogues and to question publically whether they had been dealing with co-equal concerns. Rabbi Tannenbaum, in his concluding remarks to those as-sembled at the meeting, added, "No future Jewish-Christian dialogue will take place without Jews insisting upon the confrontation on the part of Chris-tians of the profound historical, religious, cultural and liturgical meaning of the land of Israel and of Jerusalem for the Jewish People." And Rabbi Brick-ner, quoted in the July 3 issue of *Newsweek* stated, "We probably assumed that Christians knew more about the complexities of being Jewish that they really did. In our dialogues we talked about esoteric subjects (sic) like God and conscience, but we didn't discuss the meaning of Jewish peoplehood. So when the war erupted in the Middle East, Christians did not understand that it struck at the jugular vein of Jewish existence."

The very first attempt to both reorder the agenda of the dialogues and reestablish them occurred on December 6 and 7 of that year, at Andover New-ton Seminary in Massachusetts. One of the meeting's organizers, Rabbi San-ford Seltzer, explained that previous dialogues "had failed because (they) had never really begun. We had not comprehended the heart of the other. We realized that previous attempts at dialogue had not dealt with the most basic issues of the meaning of Jewish peoplehood, the role of the land of Israel in the historic psyche of the term 'Klal Israel,' a phrase whose closest English equivalent would be the Spiritual Community of Israel."

As a result of this new insight and perhaps by pragmatic happenstance, the dialogue participants began to address the differences between the two Struc-tural frameworks that caused the initial breakdown in communications. Div-idends from these new dialogues in the form of improved understanding of Judaism by the Christian clergy became evident in 1973 with the outbreak of hostilities once again between Israel and her Arab neighbors. Although the re-action of most churches was still limited, the reaction of the church leaders, who had been in dialogue since 1967, was swift and supportive. Their re-sponse to calls for support for Israel by their rabbinic colleagues gave evidence of their far greater appreciation of Jewish sentiment and concern for the State of Israel than had been the case six years earlier. As illustration, the Rev. Malcolm Boyd, an Episcopal clergyman, declared, "Christians betrayed Jews in both America and Israel at the time of the Six Day War in 1967 by failing to offer them full and unequivocal support in the moment of crisis. This failure must not be repeated by Christians again." And Father John Paw-likowski, Professor of Social Ethics at the Catholic Theological Union, pledged that "unlike the 1940's and 1967, Christians will not be silent at this time . . . Our call for peace includes a firm belief that the people of Israel must have secure boundaries for their national existence." The 1973 reaction even reflected Christian theological concerns as indicated by the statement of Father Alex Brunette, "The relationship of the Jewish people to the land of

Israel is the second area of special concern in the dialogue. This is not just a political or ethnic problem; rather it is seen as a theological reality of Jewish belief. The Promised Land of Israel in the Hebrew Scriptures and the Faith understanding of the Jewish People is an essential part of the Covenant fulfillment."

While there have been vast improvements in the appreciation of Christian leaders about the role and function of Israel within the Jewish understanding of Religion, for those who have not been involved in the dialogues, the initial confusion continues. That is where an awareness of the structural approach to religion can be most helpful. When applied to the areas of misunderstanding, such as the Christian reaction to the Six Day War, it can shed light on why the differences exist, how they can be addressed, as well as how an increased appreciation of them can develop.

NOTES

1. Michael B. Oren, *Six Days of War* (Oxford: Oxford University Press, 2002).

Chapter Six

The Role of God in the Structure

According to the Structure, in neither Judaism nor Christianity is God the Essential Element. As we indicated in chapter two, in Judaism that component of the religious Structure is the historic Jewish People while in Christianity it is Christ. At the same time, we placed a parenthesis next to each of these Essential Elements into which we inserted God in some way. For Judaism, it was a relationship to God harkening back to the events of Mount Sinai; in Christianity, it was God as an inseparable part of the Trinity. In this chapter we want to consider what happens when we remove the parentheses, when the Essential Element in Judaism is only the Jewish People but without any relationship to God, and when the Essential Element in Christianity becomes only Christ but not God.

JEWISH ATHEISM

Today there are many Jews who view themselves as atheists, who openly deny any relationship to God in their lives, who pay no heed to traditional Jewish beliefs or ideas about God, who never attend worship or do anything that is commonly understood as "religious." And yet at the same time, these people may vehemently affirm that they are Jews and bristle at any suggestion that they are anything other.

"How can this be? How can there be Jewish atheists?" the Christian will ask. It does not make sense! The answer is simple and at the same time confusing.

In sharp contrast, within Christianity faith or belief in Christ plays an indispensable role in defining one's religion. Without this faith or belief, it is impossible to be considered a Christian since it comprises the Bridge-Link to Christ. But as we have also seen, within Judaism faith-belief does not play the same function. It is not what one believes that brings a Jew into or keeps him out of his religion. The belief component appears in the Jewish Structure as a Ray after one becomes a Jew. Thus, we find Jews who profess a strong conscious self-identity as Jews but who, for whatever personal reasons, do not maintain a relationship to God as the Structure might suggest. They are what we would call "Jewish atheists," Jewish non-believers in God.

For the Christian, this Jewish designation is an anomaly. How can one be a part of a religion and at the same time declare himself an atheist? Even for the "religious" Jew, the Jewish atheist denies an important aspect of his religion. Nonetheless, the question persists: How can a Jew reject a relationship to God and simultaneously consider himself a Jew? Contrary to Christianity and peculiar to Judaism, the Jewish Structure permits this "anomaly." Identification with the Jewish People suffices for the Jewish atheist, while identification with the theological implications is not "essential." Although we have considered this type of person in an earlier chapter, we need to restate it here in order to enter into a consideration of a fascinating movement in modern Christian history, in which a group of American Christian theologians attempted to remove God from serious consideration as a part of their Essential Element. Not surprisingly, this effort elicited some intense emotional reactions and responses within Christianity, where it occurred, and a limited response within Judaism, which was an observer.

"DEATH OF GOD" THEOLOGY

Our illustration involves the very volatile but brief controversy surrounding the "Death of God" theology that occurred from the mid 1960s to the early 1970s. This example pinpoints, for our purposes, the place of belief in God within both Judaism and Christianity. Furthermore, like the illustration of the Six Day War, this controversy is well documented.

First, we need to explain the intention of the "Death of God" theology. Primarily it was an attempt on the part of a few radical Christian thinkers to respond to the secularism of their day. Harvey Cox, professor at Harvard Divinity School, in his famous book, *The Secular* City, defined secularization as "the loosing of the world from religion and quasi-religious understanding of itself, the dispelling of all closed world views, the breaking of all supernatural myths and sacred symbols." In short, modern people no longer need God "to explain, govern or justify" any dimensions of life. The phrase "Death of God," borrowed from the nineteenth century German philosopher, Friedrich

Nietzsche, was selected not only for its radical conclusion, but also for its shock value. This phrase assured public reaction which they coveted. It even earned them a cover story in the April 8, 1966 issue of *Time* magazine.

Reactions to the "Death of God" theology movement occurred in three significant areas. Two of them were in Christianity (that affected the Essential Element and the Bridge-Link) and one was in Judaism (that affected neither), but because they were not seen through the lens of the Structure of Religion, most people saw the responses only in theological or emotional terms. During the heat of the controversy the attention was focused on what was being said. Therefore, very little attention was paid either to why things were said as they were, or why reactions differed within Christianity and Judaism respectively. Consequently, few persons saw the significance of this debate as a reflection of the differences in the inherent Structure of these two religions.

The movement began in 1961 with the publication of Gabriel Vahanian's book, *The Death of God*, in which he introduced the basic concepts. His book did not attract immediate attention. Neither the *Religion Index* nor the *Catholic Periodical Literature Index* listed any articles on the topic in their 1963–64 edition. However, the former listed 33 articles on the topic in their 1965–1966 edition, with a decreasing number until 1975–1976 when only 12 articles were listed. The latter listed 21 articles in its 1965–1966 edition and by 1975–1976 it no longer had any articles. In little more than a decade, the controversy had run its course.

In addition to Vahanian, the other leading Christian exponents of this radical theology were Thomas J. J. Altizer of Emory University, William Hamilton of Colgate Rochester Divinity School, and Paul van Buren of Temple University. Each wrote extensively on their respective perception of the demise of God and how it related to the human situation of their time, a post-Holocaust world. Our concern is not with the merits or specific content of what they had to say. That we leave to theologians to evaluate.[1] What we shall treat are the public manifestations of this controversy, because they illustrate so very well the differences in the specific Structures of Judaism and Christianity.

First, we consider how the "Death of God" theology relates to the Essential Element of Christianity, that is, Christ. What did not occur is what we would term the "Unseparated Siamese Twin Reaction." By this we mean that if one of two unseparated Siamese twins dies, the second will die shortly thereafter. Because Siamese twins share organs and therefore cannot exist independently of each other, they are not distinct physical entities.

Traditional Christian theology proclaims a triune God. God the Father, God the Son (Christ), and God the Holy Spirit are in essence one and inseparable. A person cannot remove one part of this Trinity from the others and continue to maintain the orthodox Christian understanding of God. As a consequence, it follows that if God dies, so too must Christ and the Holy Spirit, since they are not independent of each other. Rather, they are united as one.

Yet the "Death of God" theologians separated God from Christ and the Holy Spirit. They openly declared that God was "dead." However, they insisted that Christ be retained. Just a few examples from this literature will illustrate what these theologians proposed. Jackson Lee Ice and John J. Carey in their book *The Death of God Debate* wrote that "We are in quest of the 'death of God' theology, a theology expressing and recording a faith which can live in Christ even following, and perhaps as a consequence of, the death of the Christian God." Thomas J. J. Altizer, who became the leading proponent of this movement, wrote in *Toward a New Christianity*, "It is the radical Christian proclamation of the death of God which liberates the Christian from every alien and lifeless image of Christ," and "when the Christian bets that God is dead, he is betting upon the real and actual presence of the fully incarnate Christ. Thus the Christian wager upon the death of God is a wager upon the presence of the living Christ, a bet that Christ is now at least potentially present in a new and total form."

Many of their Christian colleagues passionately disagreed with the so-called separation of the Trinity into a "dead God" and "living Christ." Thomas Ogletree, in *The Death of God Controversy*, wrote, "If Jesus and the events associated with his name cease to have a transcendent significance in theological reflection, the most essential (sic) basis for Christian thinking about God has been surrendered." And Larry Shiner, quoted in *The Christian Century* declared, "For to get rid of God and keep a 'Jesus ethic' of involvement with the present human situation is a species of absent-mindedness amazing to behold that takes its motto from Nietzsche. *He* at least knew better; he never tired of pointing out Christianity is a whole and that one cannot give up faith in God and keep Christian morality."[2]

These two theologians, and many other Christian thinkers who shared this response to the "Death of God" theology, intuitively understood the Structure. They fully realized that God had to remain a part of the Essential Element. Even some Jews understood this connection. Rabbi Eugene Borowitz commented on the Christian discussion of this subject when he wrote in response to their statement: "The time of the death of God is also the time of the obedience to Jesus . . . This, of course, is (their) claim to membership in the church, to the right of the title Christian. But, if (they have) no accessibility to God the Father, why (do they) affirm the special relationship to Jesus?"

As we reflect on the controversy that the "Death of God" theologians elicited, we need to ask several questions: Why did they feel a need to retain Christ? If God was dead for them, why not Christ also? Why not forsake

Christ, deny Christianity, and become deists or humanists? There are at least two possible reasons for their inability to deny the entire Trinity, which become clear when we view them through the eyes of our structural framework.

First, we may suppose that none of these theologians could follow the "Unseparated Siamese Twin Reaction" to its logical conclusion and proclaim that if God is truly dead, then Christ must be dead, too. For whatever reason, they were unable to admit that God and Christ are inseparable, and that to reject one part of the Trinity would necessitate the demise of the other two parts as well. Apparently such a final step would have been unthinkable for them; it would have been too radical! When we view this self-imposed limitation in the light of the framework, we can grasp the "reality" that they could not face. It was permissible to "kill" God, but for them also to deny Christ would have meant that they had deliberately and permanently abandoned Christianity. They would have become former-Christians, or non-Christians, which apparently was a choice that they were not ready or able to make. They still considered themselves "Christian" theologians and understood (though perhaps subconsciously) the Christian Structure. They felt compelled to promulgate their views within this religious frame of reference and ostensibly remain within Christianity. Although part of the Trinity, God, who is parenthetical within the Essential Element, was dead; Christ, who is the Essential Element, must live.

We may speculate that there was a second reason for retaining Christ in their pronouncements, and again we cannot assume that it was a conscious decision. They wanted to be heard; they needed an audience. Had they removed Christ from what they were saying, they would have lost their Christian audience. Serious Christians would have paid no attention to their message because, as noted above, they would have been speaking as former-Christians or non-Christians. They knew that in order for them to have the impact that they desired, they had to retain Christ in their theology. Again, the Essential Element of the Structure surfaces. God, who is in parenthesis, might have died for them; but Christ had to remain. This radical theology could sacrifice God only because it affirmed Jesus. Without Christ, they could not have labeled their message as Christian.

In neither instance should we see anything devious or deceptive in what the "Death of God" theologians said, even though we may disagree with them. In order to make their point, they had to say what they said in the way in which they did because of the very nature of the Christian Structure. They were a product of the Structure and had to function within it as Christians, which they freely admitted.

The second part of the Christian Structure that the "Death of God" theology affected was the Bridge-Link. This is the emotionally laden component of the Structure and it was seriously threatened by this controversy.

In order to understand the reaction of many Christians to this theology, we need to examine briefly how people in general handle disagreements. We know from our own experience and observation that when two people have a serious argument, that the most effective way in which one person can prevent himself from hearing what the other has to say is to outshout the other person. We easily recognize this behavior in such situations as a form of defense, but it is generally exhibited as a counterattack, in response to what is being said. From sports we know that the best defense is a good offense, and the outshouting of one's opponent fits that description.

Similarly, this was one reaction that many Christians had to the "Death of God" theology. They subconsciously knew the Christian Structure and realized quite correctly that if God is dead, then Christ must be dead also. Such a possibility is extremely upsetting and therefore can be threatening. Intuitively they understood that their theological system could collapse. Consequently, many Christians reacted in what they thought was an appropriate and effective manner. They tried to "outshout" the "Death of God" theologians and thereby protect their Bridge-Link of Faith-Belief. In short, these Christians counterattacked by affirming their own belief that God was not dead, and, as a consequence, neither was Christ. God was very much alive and meaningful to them as a part of the Trinity.

Protestors against the "Death of God" theologians included some prominent Christian thinkers. James D. Bales, a professor of religion at Harding University, labeled Altizer (by 1967 the major proponent of this theology) a non-Christian and dismissed all of the "Death of God" theologians in a similar fashion. The College of Bishops of the Methodist Church, Southeastern Jurisdiction, declared that Altizer "challenges the basic affirmations of every church in Christendom," and in essence they too tried to read him out of Christianity.

But far more illustrative of the degree of Christian emotion which the "Death of God" theology elicited was the reaction which occurred among some lay people. This response also makes sense in light of the Christian Structure. Two excellent examples were reported in the *Christian Advocate* of September 8, 1966. One was a "Christ-in" in Hollywood, California, in which 200 people marched carrying banners proclaiming that God was still alive. The other occurred in Miami, Florida, where a group of businessmen erected a billboard proclaiming, "God is alive. We know. He spoke with us today." Other groups of concerned Christians purchased time on television stations and used this medium to broadcast similar messages. And thousands of Christians, reacting on a very personal level, felt compelled to proclaim publicly that God was not "dead" by placing bumper stickers on their cars declaring that God was alive and well.

At this point we need to ask, does God really need this form of media publicity and advertising? Does the Divine need marches and billboards, "Christ-ins," TV commercials and bumper stickers? We can assume that God does not, since the Eternal One can manage quite well without them. God has for centuries! Who then needs them? People. Particularly people who feel seriously threatened by the very suggestion that God, and thus Christ, is dead. Their strategy was to "outshout" and thus not hear those theologians who were promulgating such threats. Hence, they spent their money and time in a fashion which they, as Christians, considered both appropriate and effective.

When we evaluate these responses,[3] they make perfect sense within the Christian Structure. Since the emotionally laden Bridge-Link of Faith-Belief was seriously challenged by these theologians—the death of God, and by implication the death of Christ—these individuals, clergy and laity alike, had to defend the Essential Element of their religion.

We now move from Christianity to Judaism and find that, to a marked degree, most Jewish thinkers did not find the "Death of God" theology a Jewish concern. The *Index of Jewish Periodicals* listed little more than a dozen articles on the subject from 1964 to 1971, not a significant number by any standard. Altizer, in his 1967 book, *Toward a New Christianity*, listed only six Jewish writers who had published anything on the subject and hoped that Judaism could "produce a fully secular faith." For the most part, the vast majority of the respondents in the symposium on the "State of Jewish Belief" in the August 1966 issue of *Commentary* magazine were typical of the Jewish reactions to this controversy. They agreed that it was "primarily a Christian problem," "strictly an internal Christian affair," and as Rabbi Norman Lamm concluded, did not believe that "the entire issue (had) any relevance to Judaism" at all. This same sentiment was echoed by Rabbi Mordecai Kaplan who stated, "Rabbis who are likely to imitate the Christian Death of God theologians should be made to realize the irrelevance of the question which has of late been agitating those Christian theologians."

However, not all Jewish thinkers agreed with Kaplan. Richard Rubenstein, author of *After Auschwitz* and the most prominent rabbi involved in the controversy, was convinced that the "problems implicit in the death of God theology (concerned) Judaism as well as Christianity," though technically the problems reflected "the Christian tradition of the passion of Christ." More pointedly, Rubenstein denied that Christianity had the ability to know that God was dead. "Nevertheless," he concluded, "I am compelled to say that we live in the time of the 'death of God.' This is more a statement about man and his culture than about God." Extrapolating from the theme of his book, he connected God's demise with the Holocaust and our living in a time "after Auschwitz." For Rubenstein, belief in a redeeming God of history, who will usher in a satisfactory end to the vicissitudes of the human condition, was no longer possible. Although Rubenstein affirmed that "in Judaism God simply does not die," he admitted that Jews living in modern times share the "radical secularity" of Christians. However, Rubenstein expressed his ultimate displeasure with many of the "Death of God" theologians when he declared, "If I am a Death of God theologian, it is with a cry of agony." In spite of his interest in and sympathy for this discussion, Rubenstein could not be a full participant in the movement.

Perhaps the most telling Jewish reaction to this controversy was found at the end of an article in the Winter 1966 issue of *Judaism* which was subsequently reprinted in an anthology of the "Death of God" literature. In it, Rabbi Eugene Borowitz reviewed some of the current literature on the subject so that if any Jews found themselves in a situation where the "Death of God" movement was being discussed they might be conversant on the subject. Almost as a postscript to his review, he wrote: "I confess that I do not see much for Judaism to learn from the current Protestant discussion, though a new style for communicating old truths would be useful. It all sounds so familiar. The haskalah literature is full of the death of God and religion because we have reached the age of science. Our Yiddishists and Hebraists substitute culture for religion; our Zionists and socialists have made it politics; Felix Adler tried ethics; and a continuing host try the arts, university, research and self-indulgence. Anyone who wants to see what putting religion into secular terms is can come to us for living examples. In the State of Israel we have it in power; in *Commentary* magazine it stamps secular intellectuality indelibly on urban American culture."[4]

The major difference between these tepid Jewish reactions and the heated Christian reactions was involvement. For Jews, the "Death of God" controversy was simply not a Jewish problem. Although this ambivalence can be elaborated in theological terms, as some of the *Commentary* respondents did, that is not enough. We need to contextualize Jewish non-involvement by setting it in the framework of Borowitz' comment that there are Jewish secularists and atheists.

When these Jewish reactions to the "Death of God" theology are placed into the Jewish Structure, we see that they make sense. What a person believes or does not believe about God is not part of the Jewish Bridge-Link that brings that individual into his Religion. For Jews, that is the function of one's Conscious Self-Identification. As we saw in our consideration of Jewish religious ideas, they occur in the realm of the Rays that emanate from Judaism. They are not the Bridge-Link, as they are in Christianity.

In the *Commentary* symposium, Rabbi Solomon B. Freehof stated this difference in terms of the structural Framework very succinctly. He wrote, "The

'God is Dead' question agitating the so-called 'radical Christians' is of comparatively small relevance for Judaism. For a number of reasons this agitation has little meaning for us. If a Christian ceases to believe in God, he ceases to be a Christian and may be completely lost to the church. If a Jew becomes an atheist, he is still in many ways Jewish and his children will be among those who found synagogues. Since we do not lose our fellow Jews quite so easily, we have no reason to panic." Christians, however, could not emotionally, theologically, or structurally endorse any ambivalence or ambiguity in belief as the "Death of God" theologians espoused.

In conclusion, these three aspects of the "Death of God" theology—the lack of the "Unseparated Siamese Twin Reaction," the emotional reaction of many Christians to this controversy, and the general indifference toward it among leading Jewish thinkers and Jews in general—went unnoticed at the time because they were not placed within the context of the Structure of Religion. However, when we view them today from our vantage point of time, we see that all three of these reactions are excellent examples of the way in which the Structural framework operates in both Christianity and Judaism. In Christianity, they highlight the centrality of Christ, the indispensability of God as part of the Trinity, and the emotional nature of Faith-Belief. In Judaism, they illustrate that theological differences are not an emotional issue, as well as the fact that Judaism can include secularists and atheists. These are crucial differences in function between the two religions that are often misunderstood but which the Structure can easily explain.

NOTES

1. See Thomas W. Ogletree, *The Death of God Controversy* (Nashville, TN: Abingdon Press, 1966) and Stephen R. Haynes and John R. Roth, eds., *The Death of God Movement and the Holocaust: Radical Theology Encounters the Shoah* (Westport, CT: Greenwood Press, 1999).

2. Larry Shiner, "Goodbye, Death-of-God!" *The Christian Century* (November 17, 1965): 1418.

3. It is important to note that African American theologians in general did not participate in this debate. Hubert G. Locke observes "that the proclamation of God's death came in the midst of a decade in which black Americans were giving powerful expression to the opposite conviction." The civil rights struggle was rooted in the liberating God of history whom the radical theologians denied.

4. Eugene Borowitz, "God-Is-Dead Theology" in *The Meaning of the Death of God: Protestant, Jewish and Catholic Scholars Explore Atheistic Theology*, ed. Bernard Murchland (New York: Random House, 1967), 106.

Part Two

DISCUSSION QUESTIONS

Introduction to Part Two

Now that the reader has completed part one, we think it is beneficial to present a series of questions that highlight subtle as well as significant differences between the two religions. Moreover, there are still many topics, which the text does not cover, that may create confusion or misunderstanding for the Jew or Christian reading about either religion. Therefore, we encourage the use of this part of the book for individual learning, as well as group discussion.

We have identified a limited number of questions that will expand the reader's knowledge of both religions. Some of them are theological, which part one deliberately omitted; some of them are more historical; while others treat functional differences. They are intended to address differences between the two religions that were not germane to our presentation of the Structural approach. Some of the responses to these questions are short and rather straightforward because of the nature of the questions themselves. Other responses are much longer because particular questions are more complicated and require a more detailed reply. The latter are primarily questions that are asked of Christianity. You will note that we have described this part as "a Jewish" and "a Christian" response to questions asked. Although our answers are representative of our respective traditions, we acknowledge the diversity inherent in both religions. Therefore, our responses are neither definitive nor singular. Rather, they are intended to inform and stimulate.

We hope that this part of the book will encourage further reflection and open dialogue. In addition, we assume that the subject matter of the questions will be more easily understood as a result of the reader's knowledge of the Structure and how it functions within each religious tradition.

A JEWISH RESPONSE TO QUESTIONS
CHRISTIANS ASK JEWS

Question One: Why Don't Jews Believe in Jesus as the Messiah?

Since, as our book explains in chapter one, historic Rabbinic Judaism did not accept the claims of Jesus as the Messiah, Jesus does not hold the same position in Judaism as he does in Christianity.

And as chapter one explains also, both religions come out of the Pharisaic tradition of the time of the Second Temple, each going its own way independent of the other as "fraternal twins." Thus we find two separate post-Biblical traditions—one Jewish and the other Christian, each with its own holidays, beliefs, and ways of doing things.

But perhaps the easiest way to indicate why Judaism pays not attention to Jesus is to make the comparison with Mohammed. Neither Judaism nor Christianity pays any attention to him within their traditions—though millions of Muslims do. Mohammed is not a part of either Jewish or Christian tradition. In the same way Jesus is not a part of Jewish tradition. He is only a part of the Christian tradition. Thus we find two different traditions and what is central to one tradition, Jesus as the Christ, is not even considered or a part of the other.

Question Two: What is the Jewish View of the Messiah?

Because Jewish Religious Ideas are not definitive in the same way that Christian theology tends to be, it is impossible to give a specific Jewish belief concerning the Messiah. Thus one can only deal in generalities.

The Jewish idea of the Messiah is based on a number of passages in Scripture, however perhaps the best illustration is found in Isaiah 2:4 which states:

And He shall judge between the nations,
And shall decide for many peoples;
And they shall beat their swords into plowshares,
And their spears into pruning-hooks;
Nation shall not lift up sword against nation,
Neither shall they learn war any more.

As a result, the Jewish view of the Messiah is this world-centered in contrast to Christianity which has viewed the Messiah as being a person who has accepted the sins of the world upon himself and leads the believer to a favorable situation in the after life. In very sharp contrast, the Jewish Messiah is expected to bring about an era of universal peace and well-being to this world, in an almost Utopian fashion, harkening back to the days in the Garden of Eden.

Historically, the Messiah was also expected to be a descendant of King David, the greatest of the Biblical monarchs, a view which Christianity picked up as we see in the genealogy of Jesus at the beginning of the Gospel of Matthew.

Other hopes were also connected with the coming of the Messiah, such as all Jews—both living and dead—would somehow return to the Land of Israel. The specifics of when this would happen and how it would take place were left up to God, as were many of the details concerning the events of that wonderful, far off time.

While this belief was not spelled out within Judaism, it was continually present in the *Aleynu*, one of the concluding prayers in the Jewish worship service, as well as the words, "Next year in Jerusalem," found at the conclusion of the Passover Seder and day long worship on Yom Kippur, the Day of Atonement. Historically this was a "faith-centered" hope that God would bring this about. As we saw in our discussion of the modern State of Israel, it became a political reality only in modern times.

Question Three: Do Jews Use the Christian Bible?

Perhaps this question ought to be restated: Do Christians use the Jewish Bible? The Hebrew Bible is about the Jews—the history of the ancient Jewish People and their encounters with God. The accounts in this Book are about this people—the Patriarchs, Moses, the Prophets, and the other literature which they produced over a number of centuries. It was the Jewish Bible long before Christianity incorporated it into its sacred canon.

Christianity, as it developed, took this ancient Jewish text, added its own Scriptures to it (the New Testament), and interpreted it to predict the coming of Jesus as the Messiah. What Christians call the Old Testament is really the Jewish Bible. Both religions utilize it, but they do so in some very different ways. There is a wealth of Jewish interpretative tradition about the Bible, known technically as the "Oral Torah," which includes the Mishnah, the two Talmuds and a vast body of midrashic (sermonic interpretation) literature. This rabbinic tradition provides the Jew with a way in which to view the text and to go beyond any literal interpretation of the words, providing an understanding based on the Hebrew text, the language in which it was originally written, in ways that are not possible in any English translation.

By contrast, a good bit of Christian understanding of the Jewish Bible is seeing it as foretelling the coming of Jesus. Thus the two religions use the same text in very different ways, each appropriate to its own tradition.

In addition, the order of the books in the Jewish Bible is different from the order in the Christian Old Testament. The Jewish order generally follows an historic development model, with the Torah (Pentateuch) first, as in the Christian Bible. The next section includes Joshua, Judges, the two books of Samuel, the two books of Kings, followed by the literary prophets. The third section is an anthology, starting with Psalms and followed by other later books, concluding with the two books of Chronicles. The Christian order, because it is messianically oriented, has the prophetic books at the end, leading the reader into the New Testament and its accounts of Jesus' life found in the Gospels.

Question Four: Why Don't Jews Celebrate Christmas?

Christmas is strictly a Christian holiday, commemorating the birth of Jesus. Since Jesus is not a part of Jewish tradition, Jews see no reason to observe this holiday. It is not theirs, in the same way that folks of both religions do not celebrate Ramadan, a Moslem holiday.

Question Five: Do Jews Still Use Sacrifices?

The sacrificial system was the mode of worship in the Temple of old in Jerusalem, both the first one which Solomon built and the second one built in the time of Ezra and expanded upon by Herod the Great. With the destruction of the Second Temple by the Romans in 70 CE, the sacrificial system ceased. Since that time there has no longer been a place for it to occur. Consequently, the only place of Jewish worship has been the synagogue.

The New Testament tells us that both Jesus and Paul entered synagogues regularly. It is no surprise then that the church, as a worship institution, is a direct copy of the synagogue in its form of worship, which is not with sacrifices as was practiced in the Temple, but rather with words.

Question Six: What is a Synagogue?

The synagogue is the post-Biblical Jewish house of worship. However, scholars are not certain as to its origins because there is no literature extant that is conclusive in describing how this important Jewish worship institution came to be. But what we do know is that it came into existence some time prior to the time of Jesus, while the Temple was still in standing and in use. We know this because the Gospels mention numerous times that he frequented the synagogue on the Sabbath, as a Jew living in Palestine. By the time of Paul, also a Jew and a number of years later, we read that they were found throughout the Eastern Mediterranean world because Acts informs us that he preached in them.

The mode of worship in the synagogue is with words—prayers, songs, Bible readings and sermons. This is the model after which Christian worship was patterned. As a result the general format of worship is the same in both a synagogue and a church. The differences are in the specifics of the service and the words which are spoken

Question Seven: Can Jews Be Saved?

This is a Christian question and is of far less concern to Jews. As our text indicates, the word "salvation" has a totally different meaning between the two religions.

Because traditional Christianity has focused in on the believer achieving a favorable place in the life after death as the meaning of "salvation," this has become a major consideration for many Christians, and as our text points out, historically was the reason put forth for becoming a Christian. It has been the major thrust of the evangelical message.

In sharp contrast it is not a major concern for Jews. Far more important is how we live our lives here on earth in order to sanctify one's every day existence (see Leviticus 19). What happens after this life Jews leave to God. It is His decision and we ought not try to second guess Him.

Furthermore, a belief in an after life is just that—a belief, even a hope. It is not provable in the way in which we normally seek the proof of something of a more physical nature. Nonetheless, this hope is found within Judaism and is mentioned specifically in the *El Male Rachamim* (Oh God full of mercies) prayer recited at the conclusion of a funeral service. But there is very little mention of the after life within the worship service *per se*, except a brief reference in one of the prayers (the Gevurot of the Amidah) to God reviving the dead and in a preliminary prayer referring to God restoring souls to the dead. Reform Judaism has changed the Hebrew wording of the former prayer, removing this reference and substituted that God gives life to all.

Again, we encounter two different religions with two different traditions about the after life. We need to recognize each as appropriate within its own context.

Question Eight: What Then Do Jews Believe about After Life?

There is no specific mention of an after life *per se* in the Jewish Bible. It is a post-Biblical belief, read back into the Bible by the rabbis and done by quoting passages (a method known as proof-texting) to support it.

Because Jewish religious ideas are not definitive, there is not one Jewish view on an after life. Nonetheless, after life is discussed in rabbinic literature with three good places to go and one not so good place. How one ends up in which depends on how he has lived his life. Again, as indicated above, a concern for the after life is not a major theme for Jews as it is among some Christians. However, it ought to be pointed out, that the Jewish view of an after life does not exclude non-Jews. Rather, all righteous people, regardless of religious belief, can have a share in the after life, often referred to also as "the world to come." Thus the Jewish after life, as non-defined as it is, is not as exclusive as the Christian belief, which is based on one's faith in Jesus as the Christ.

Question Nine: Why is the Jewish Calendar so Peculiar?

The secular calendar is a solar calendar. The sun dictates both the years and the months.

The Jewish calendar is a solar-lunar calendar. The years are determined by the sun—so that the holiday of Passover is always in the spring and the holiday of Sukkot is always in the fall.

However, the moon determines the months. Every new moon marks the beginning of a new Jewish month, each with its own Hebrew name. Thus there are 28 days in each month, the time span from new moon to new moon. Such an arrangement needs correcting every few years in order to keep the lunar months in proper relationship to the solar year. As a result there is an extra month added to the calendar every few years, in a regular cycle.

Christmas is always on December 25th. However, the date of Easter is different every year. This is because, according to the Gospel accounts, the crucifixion occurred during Passover. The Church wanted to maintain this connection for theological reasons, Jesus being considered the sacrifice of the Pascal lamb. Thus the holiday was tied to the Jewish calendar by a peculiar formula in order to retain this historic connection and for it to be observed in the spring. The formula is that Easter falls on the first Sunday, after the first full moon, after the spring equinox. This is a rather convoluted way of setting a date, but one that was necessary in order to maintain the historic tie. It usually works, except when Easter comes almost immediately after the equinox and Judaism has a leap year, having added an additional month at that season in order to get the lunar and the solar year back in proper relationship.

Question Ten: What Holidays do Jews Observe?

Jews have far more holidays than do Christians. There are three Pilgrim Festivals and two High Holidays which are all mentioned in the text of the

Torah—the Pentateuch, the Five Books of Moses—and which are called major holidays as a result, though the observance of them today is far different from what we read in Scripture.

The Pilgrim Festivals are Pesach (Passover), Shavuot (Pentecost) and Sukkot (the Festival of Booths). Each of these is connected with the agricultural year in Scripture, and two of them with other events as well.

Pesach was the holiday of the winter grain harvest and of the spring lambs—as symbolized by the matzah (unleavened bread) and the Paschal lamb mentioned in the book of Exodus. Both of these symbols have been maintained and are represented on the Seder plate at the Seder (the ritual meal celebrated within a family setting for the holiday, a meal which is wrapped around a liturgical worship service held at the family dinner table). This holiday commemorates the Exodus of the Children of Israel from Egypt, with its central theme being that of freedom from slavery, redemption in the Jewish usage of the word.

Shavuot was the holiday of the first fruits of the spring planting but has also become associated with the giving of the Torah at Mt. Sinai because it occurs in the third month after the Exodus, as the Torah tells us that the Children of Israel came to that mountain in the third month. In modern times, many Reform and Conservative congregations (see next question) hold Confirmation ceremonies during this holiday, when Jewish young people publicly symbolize their acceptance of the Torah for themselves.

Sukkot is the festival of the fall harvest. It is observed with the construction of temporary shelters (called a sukkah, the plural being sukkot) in which meals are often taken. There are additional symbols used in this holiday observance—a lulav (a palm frond with a twig of myrtle and willow bound to its base), and an etrog (a lemon-like citron). The holiday does not mark any specific historic event within Jewish history. However the reading of the annual Torah cycle both ends and begins during this holiday, with Simchat Torah at its conclusion. It is a time of great rejoicing in the synagogue, when the scrolls of the Torah are paraded around the sanctuary with much festivity, and with a great deal of singing and dancing. The last verses of Deuteronomy are read followed immediately by the reading of the opening verses of Genesis, so that there is a never ending tradition of reading from those five books.

The High Holidays, which usually occur in early fall, are Rosh Hashanah (the Jewish New Year) and, ten days later, Yom Kippur (the Day of Atonement). Both of these holidays are synagogue centered and observed with solemn worship. It is believed that the Book of Life is opened on Rosh Hashanah and sealed on Yom Kippur, indicating who will live and who will die during the coming year. Both holidays are times of serious introspection, of contrition, of soul searching and trying to make amends for the sins and shortcomings of the previous year. Many of the prayers recited have these themes and are intended to help the worshipper to review his life and see where and how he can come closer to the way in which God would have him live. Yom Kippur, which is the more somber of the two holidays, is a twenty-four hour fast day, with the belief that forgoing food helps the individual focus on his sins rather than his physical needs.

There are numerous other Jewish holidays, considered minor holidays because they are not mentioned in the Torah. The two most significant of these are Hanukkah and Purim.

Purim is based on the Book of Esther, found in the Bible. This book is the story of Queen Esther and her successful attempt to prevent Haman, the Prime Minister of Persia, from destroying the Jews of that ancient kingdom because Mordecai, her uncle, refused to bow down to Haman as he rode through the streets of the capital city. It is a tale of the salvation (a Jewish use of the word) of the Jews from certain destruction by a megalomaniacal enemy, the prototype of many tales of similar nature in the history of Judaism. It is celebrated in the synagogue by the reading of the Book of Esther, with great noise at the mention of the villain Haman, and with much merry making. In addition there is a special, triangular, filled pastry, Hamantaschen, served as part of the observance

Hanukkah, the origins of which are found in the Books of Maccabees, two books which are in the Apocrypha, a collection of post biblical literature found in the Catholic Old Testament but not in either the Hebrew Bible or the Protestant Old Testament. It is based on the story of the struggle of a group of Jews, lead by Judas Maccabeus, against Antiochus Epiphanes, the Greek oriented Syrian king, to stamp out Judaism within his realm. Judas and his followers triumphed over Antiochus and rededicated the Temple in Jerusalem (the name Hanukkah means dedication). According to the legend, he found a small jar of pure olive oil there, enough believed to last only one day, but which miraculously lasted eight days. Thus it is an eight day observance, primarily in the home with the lighting of an increasing number of candles each night. The theme of the holiday is that of religious freedom.

Among the lesser Jewish holidays are Tu'b'Shevat (the New Year of the Trees), Tisha b'Av (a fast day marking the destruction of both Temples) and a number of other observances as well.

Question Eleven: What is the Difference Between Orthodox, Conservative and Reform Judaism?

These three movements within Judaism are of fairly modern origins, coming out of the Enlightenment in Europe beginning in the late Eighteenth Century. Prior to that time, there were no such distinctions within Judaism.

Orthodox Judaism claims to maintain Jewish tradition as it always was, that it is true to both the Torah and rabbinic tradition throughout the ages. One of its major foci is the maintenance of Halachah, Jewish law. Thus the daily life of the Orthodox Jew is generally directed by traditional Jewish practice and this regimen is found in every aspect of his life, from the time he arises in the morning until he retires a night. It affects his eating habits, his family relationships, the ceremonies and rituals he and his family observe, and everything else that is part of his daily routine. As we mentioned within the text of this book, for him Judaism is a "Way of Life" based on an ancient tradition believed to have been handed down by God at Mt. Sinai, both in written form (the Written Torah) and orally (the Oral Torah).

Conservative Judaism is in the middle of the spectrum. It is more liberal in its interpretation of Jewish tradition and of the biblical literature, willing to see human input into it, as well as God. On the other hand, it is still Halachically oriented, wishing to observe as much of Jewish law as feasible, while at the same time bending a bit to modern ways. Its worship in general still maintains the orthodox patterns, though there have been a few changes within the service. Conservative Judaism developed in this country as a counter to Reform and as a way of appealing to Jews who were no longer comfortable within Orthodoxy but could not accept the changes which Reform had instituted.

Reform Judaism began in the early 19th century in Germany, with the breakdown of the ghettoes that segregated Jews from the general populace. It started among Jews who wanted to appear more German in their worship, with the introduction of sermons in German in the synagogue, hymns in German, the use of an organ in the synagogue, as well as abbreviating the lengthy traditional Sabbath worship service. Many of the Jews from Germany who came to this country in the mid-nineteenth century brought these ideas with them and established Reform synagogues in the United States. The worship patterns of Reform have changed greatly since that time, but the underlying belief that Judaism is able to change with the times and adapt to new ideas and beliefs, while still maintaining a strong identity with the Jewish People, remains.

Reform Judaism is the liberal branch of Judaism in America. It views Jewish tradition, both the Bible and post-biblical literature, as a product of human endeavor and divine inspiration, though unwilling to define which part is which. It is less concerned about Jewish law and observance, and more focused on social action and ethical behavior, both private and public.

A CHRISTIAN RESPONSE TO QUESTIONS
JEWS ASK CHRISTIANS

Question One: Was Jesus Resurrected from the Dead?

For the Christian, this is the most basic question you can ask. According to the church, the resurrection of Jesus from the dead affirms Jesus as the Christ—the Essential Element of Christianity. This question also invites inquiry into what happened on Easter Day and why Christianity began. But most important, this question locates the heart of the Christian tradition. Without the resurrection of Jesus, there would be no religion called Christianity.

Although the resurrection of Jesus represents the watershed event for the New Testament, it is not described in any of the early church writings. There is a tradition of empty tomb accounts, but there are no "exit from the tomb" stories. Thus, the resurrection, while described as a "real" event by the New Testament writers, is not like any other event in time and space. As the inaugural moment of God's new creation, it signals for Christians the great divide between the "fallen" present age and the "redeemed" age to come. Since faith and history meet at the resurrection, a description of this "transhistorical" event, let alone its full meaning, eludes both historians and theologians.

In the Apostles' Creed, formulated in the second century, the church declares that Jesus was an ordinary person who experienced both birth and death. Yet he was also an extraordinary person because he had a "unique prehistory" ("conceived by the Holy Spirit") and an "unusual posthistory" ("on the third day he was raised from the dead").

The early Christian confession that Jesus rose from the dead must be understood against the backdrop of Jewish understandings of resurrection at the time of Jesus. Evidence in the Hebrew Scriptures for Jewish belief in the concept of resurrection is ambiguous. Although several passages allude to God's power over death (Deuteronomy 32:39, I Samuel 2:6, and Isaiah 25:7–8), Psalm 115:17 suggests that God lacks power over death. The first unequivocal statement of belief in the resurrection of the dead is found in the apocalyptic (this genre of literature refers to God's revelation concerning the end of time) and late (most likely written during Antiochus's persecution of the Jews around 167 B.C.E.) book of Daniel 12:2: "Many of those who sleep in the dust of the earth shall awake, some to everlasting life, and some to shame and everlasting contempt."

According to the Jewish historian Josephus (37–100 C.E.), by the time of Jesus three distinct beliefs had emerged. The Sadducees (the ruling party of the Temple) and the Samaritans (descendants of the Jews who were not exiled to Babylonia, who lived north of Jerusalem, and who married non-Jews and brought elements of non-Jewish worship into their religion) denied any sort of future life. The Essenes (the "pious ones" who separated themselves from the world and awaited the end of history, and may have been the people of Qumran and the Dead Sea Scrolls) believed in the immortality of the soul but not the body, while the Pharisees (students of the scriptures and leaders of the synagogue) believed in the resurrection of the body as a communal concept for only the righteous.

In First Corinthians 15:3–8, written around 54 C.E., the only surviving account by a person who experienced firsthand an appearance of the resurrected Jesus, Paul recounts the Gospel message: "For I handed on to you as of first importance what I in turn had received; that Christ died for our sins in accordance with the scriptures, and that he was buried, and that he was raised on the third day in accordance with the scriptures, and that he appeared to Cephas, then to the twelve. Then he appeared to more than five hundred brothers and sisters at one time, most of whom are still alive, though some have died. Then he appeared to James, then to all the apostles. Last of all, as to one untimely born, he appeared also to me."

At least two Pauline convictions are significant. First, the resurrected body of Jesus possesses both continuity and discontinuity with the historical Jesus. There is continuity since Jesus' resurrected body is a "spiritual body," and therefore he is recognized in the appearance stories. The contrast is not between physical and nonphysical bodies, but rather between "a body animated by 'soul'" (a natural body) and "a body animated by 'spirit'" (and therefore transcends the natural process of decay). There is discontinuity because the resurrected body is not identical to the historical body. Like a seed that dies in order for a plant to grow (I Corinthians 15:36–37), Jesus' body is not resuscitated. It dies and is transformed (I Corinthians 15:51). Second, Paul affirms the resurrection as the definitive Christian event when he writes in I Corinthians 15:13–14: "If there is no resurrection of the dead, then Christ has not been raised, then our proclamation has been in vain, and your faith has been in vain."

Although the four canonical Gospel (see a Christian response to question #3) accounts of Easter morning (Matthew 28, Mark 16, Luke 24, and John 20) are impossible to harmonize, they nonetheless confirm Paul's continuity-discontinuity characterization. On the one hand, Jesus is recognized and touched, he cooks and eats, and, on the other hand, Jesus disappears at will, passes through locked doors, and occasionally goes unrecognized. Like Paul, the Gospel evangelists oppose the idea that the risen Lord was a ghost or an apparition (Luke 24:39), as well as the idea that Jesus was a resuscitated corpse (Mark 16:6). They all agree that he was raised from the dead by God.

These five New Testament witnesses to the resurrection contain two basic kinds of accounts: empty tomb stories and appearance stories. It is important to note the absence of an "exit story." As mentioned at the beginning of this response, there are no direct reports of Jesus leaving the tomb. All four Gospel narratives move from an account of burying Jesus in the tomb to an account of discovering an empty tomb. The resurrection, as a "transhistorical" event, eludes description.

In total, the New Testament records at least eleven different appearances of a resurrected Jesus separate from Paul. They are: to the women (Matthew 28:9–10), to Mary Magdalene (John 20:11–18), to Peter (I Corinthians 15:5, Luke 24:34, possibly Mark 16:7), to two disciples on the road to Emmaus (Luke 24:13–31), to the eleven and other disciples (accounts 5–8 are found in Luke 24:36–49 and John 20:19–23, John 20:24–29, Matthew 28:16–20, Acts 1:6–9), to seven disciples (John 21:1–14), to more than five hundred (I Corinthians 15:6), and to James (I Corinthians 15:7).

Three features are prominent. First, the common denominator in all the appearances is that they occurred to followers of Jesus. Appearance stories reassure those who had already accepted Jesus as the Messiah and are not intended to convert nonbelievers. Second, the locations of the appearances vary from Jerusalem to Galilee. Third, the forms of the appearances also differ.

In conclusion, belief in the resurrection is grounded in the conviction that Jesus lives. Because the risen Lord appeared to his followers again and again, the "truth" of the Easter story was, and is, experiential (refer to the Emmaus road account in Luke 24:13–35). As the resurrected Messiah from the dead, Jesus reversed the fall of Adam in the past (I Corinthian 15:21–22), reigns as Living Lord in the present (John 20:28), and inaugurates the future eschatological reign of God on earth (Romans 8).

Question Two: Was Jesus Born of a Virgin?

The doctrine of the "virgin birth," that Mary the mother of Jesus conceived and bore him apart from sexual intercourse with her husband Joseph, has played a disproportionately important role in the Christian tradition. Because Christmas "functions" as the major religious holiday in modern western culture, the stories of Jesus' birth have been instrumental in shaping both Christian and cultural images of Jesus.

Yet ironies exist. For example, the stories speak of the virginal "conception of Jesus," not his "virgin birth." Moreover, with the exception of the infancy narratives in the Gospels of Matthew and Luke, the New Testament is silent about this event! Not only do the Gospels of Mark and John not mention a "virgin birth," but the Pauline letters, the earliest books of the accepted Christian canon, are deafeningly quiet. Even the sermons of Peter and Paul, as reported in the book of Acts and composed by the author of Luke, are devoid of any tradition about the virginal conception.

Nonetheless, two Gospels tell the story of Jesus' "virgin birth." Matthew's story (1:18–25) serves as a theological commentary on verse 16 of the preceding genealogy: "And Jacob the father of Joseph the husband of Mary, of whom Jesus was born, who is called the Messiah." As the birth story begins in Matthew, Mary has already conceived her child and, consequently, Joseph is dismayed over her pregnancy and seeks to divorce her. An angel appears to Joseph, not Mary, and convinces him that the child is from the Holy Spirit and that he should proceed with the marriage. Thus, Joseph "adopts" the divinely conceived "Emmanuel" (verse 23) into the Davidic, royal-messianic lineage. The multiple references (note the use of proof texting) by Matthew to Hebrew prophecy fulfilled (Isaiah 7:14, 11:1, Micah 5:2, Hosea 11:1, and Jeremiah 31:15) suggest that the original audience of the story was Jewish Christians.

Luke's account of the "virgin birth" (1:26–38) is an "annunciation" story since the conception has not yet occurred. In this narrative, Mary is distraught over the angelic appearance and announcement that she, a "virgin," will conceive a son without a husband. The angel convinces her that "the Holy Spirit will come upon you" and that "the child to be born will be holy" and called the "Son of God." Unlike the Matthean story, Luke's story of Jesus' conception and birth parallels the story of the conception and birth of John the Baptist. In this way, Luke establishes Jesus' "solidarity with, but superiority to" the Baptist because John is "filled" with the Holy Spirit while Jesus is "conceived" by the Holy Spirit.

There is almost universal agreement among mainline New Testament scholars that these infancy narratives are written "in the language of piety and poetry." That is, the stories are confessional more than reliable history. According to Marcus Borg in *The Meaning of Jesus*, at least three reasons support this judgment. First, the birth tradition is "relatively late." As previously mentioned, the earlier writers of the New Testament do not refer to a supernatural conception. Paul, the earliest writer, does not, and Mark, the earliest Gospel, does not.

Second, the obvious differences between the two birth stories suggest that they are actually two distinct stories and not a single story that has been modified. For example, the locations differ significantly. In Luke, Mary and Joseph live in Nazareth but journey to Bethlehem because of the census, whereas in Matthew Mary and Joseph already live in Bethlehem where the birth occurs at home, and not in a stable. The visitors to Matthew's Jesus are "wise men from the East" who follow a star, while Luke has angels singing in the night sky to shepherds who make the pilgrimage.

Third, the birth stories were "composed to be overtures to each gospel." The theme of each nativity narrative introduces the overall portrait of Jesus found in the respective Gospel. Matthew's Jesus is "the king of the Jews" and Luke's Jesus is "a Spirit-anointed social prophet."[1]

These striking differences do not, however, diminish their similarities: Jesus was conceived by the Holy Spirit and born in Bethlehem. The former agreement is a *theological* affirmation of Jesus' relationship to God and cannot be historically verified. The latter agreement probably reflects the early Christian conviction that Jesus, the Son of David and the Messiah, needed to be born in Bethlehem because it was the ancestral home of King David. According to historians, only the following information seems reliable: Jesus was born before the death of Herod the Great in 4 B.C.E., his parents were Mary and Joseph, and the town of birth was probably Nazareth and not Bethlehem.

Although the historical accuracy of the two birth stories is problematic, the narratives assert three essential claims. First, the stories underscore the "lordship" of Jesus and thereby make a political statement. In Matthew's account, Jesus' rivalry with Herod as the rightful "king of the Jews" intentionally recalls the earlier Hebrew story of the rivalry between Pharaoh and the God of Moses. In Luke's account, the conflict is between the lordship of Caesar and of Christ. Regardless of the adversary, both Matthew and Luke affirm Jesus as the "true lord."

Second, the stories reinforce the Biblical theme that neither the Jewish nor the Christian communities can existence without God's initial and sustaining grace. Throughout the Hebrew Scriptures there are accounts of remarkable births. From Isaac, Jacob and Esau, Joseph, and including the conceptions of Samson and Samuel, the people of God are both called and supported by God's grace. Matthew and Luke continue this theme. Because God has acted anew in the birth of Jesus, the Christian community believes that it lives in grace-filled hope.

Third, and most obvious, the birth narratives declare that Jesus was "of God." Conception by the Holy Spirit affirms that Jesus was "born, not of blood or the will of the flesh or of the will of man, but of God" (John 1:13). Jesus is the Son of God precisely because he was "fathered" by God.

The story of the "virgin birth," or more accurately the virginal conception, is not a biological statement that proves Jesus was the Son of God. Rather, it affirms in narrative form the church's confession that in the life of Jesus the presence and power of God is both visible and available.

Question Three: Why are there Four Gospels and Not One?

This is an excellent question since it would seem logical that the church would want only one written Gospel to witness to the one Lord. Before a satisfactory response can be provided, however, we need to broaden the context.

It is best to think of the Christian New Testament as a collection of early church writings, rather than a single tome. Of the 27 books that comprise the New Testament, one book is historical (Acts), one book is apocalyptic (Revelation), twenty-one books are actually letters (of which fourteen are associated with the Apostle Paul), and four books are Gospels. The word "gospel" is the English translation of the Greek *euangelion*, which literally means "good news." Originally this term referred "to the message about the death, resurrection, and return of Jesus Christ" (e.g., I Corinthians 15:1–5), and only in the second century did the word "gospel" become associated with the written documents about the "good news" of Jesus' ministry.

These 27 books form what Christians call the New Testament canon. (Note that the word "canon" can also refer to the collection of books that comprise the Hebrew Bible.) By the late second century the term "canon" (which means "norm" or "standard") was used to designate the wide range of Christian teachings that were authoritative for the church's belief and practice. The earliest known use of the word "canon" for the exact 27 books of the New Testament in their current order is the Easter Letter of Athanasius, Bishop of Alexandria, in 367 C.E.

Now we are ready to address the specific question: Why four Gospels and not one? Although the history of that decision by the ancient church is obscure, there are discernible patterns. The four canonical Gospels (Matthew, Mark, Luke, and John) did not attain clear prominence until late in the second century. Several historical factors explain this late designation. First, each Gospel was initially *the* Gospel for a specific Christian community. It was local before it became universal. Second, we know that there were other Gospels besides these four. Although we shall never know exactly how many, the fact that there were more than four indicates that the identification of four canonical Gospels was the result of a selective process. In his book *The Complete Gospels*, Robert J. Miller provides the text of 17 extant Gospels. (In addition to the English translation, there is information about the author, audience, date, and theme of each Gospel.) The 13 Gospels that "did not make the cut" are called "extracanonical gospels." Third, the Marcion controversy around the middle of the second century in Rome (Marcion, a wealthy member of the Christian community in Rome, included only one Gospel [Luke] and no books from the Hebrew Scriptures in his collection of Christian Scriptures) suggests that there was no perceived need for more than one Gospel as yet.

At least three additional reasons precluded the early church from initially endorsing multiple Gospels. First, a plurality of Gospels cast doubt on the adequacy, accuracy, and authority of any one Gospel. Second, this problem was

compounded by the realization that the Gospels contained obvious and significant differences. (For example, only Matthew and Luke contained birth
stories, and they differed tremendously. See a Christian response to question
two.) Third, the term "gospel" originally applied to a theological concept
("the good news" of God's salvation available in Jesus) and not to a literary
document. According to the former concept, Christianity can have only one
gospel.

The reluctance of the early church to authorize more than one written
Gospel is also testified by the popularity of Tatian's *Diatessaron*. Writing
around 170 C.E., Tatian, a Syrian Christian, wove together separate Gospels
(using mainly but not exclusively the four Gospels that would be canonized)
into a single, harmonious Gospel. Ironically few Christians today even know
about this book.

The first evidence for a collection of the four canonical Gospels comes
from Irenaeus, Bishop of Lyons in Gaul, about 180 C.E. He argues that because there are "four zones of the world," "four principal winds," "four principal covenants," and "living creatures are quadriform," the gospel (the "good
news" of God's salvation in Jesus the Christ) should be "quadriform." His
comment indicates that toward the end of the second century the use of four
Gospels was becoming common in Western Christianity.

Although the formation of a "four Gospel" canon cannot be viewed as either necessary or natural, it represents a logical compromise between an "un-
manageable multiplicity of gospels" and "a single, self-consistent gospel."
This inherent tension can be detected in the church's insistence that there is
the Gospel of Jesus Christ (singular) in four witnesses (the four canonical
Gospels). Technically speaking there is a "fourfold gospel."

The authorization of four canonical Gospels means at least four gains for
the church. First, it increases the chances of securing historical knowledge.
The historian is better served by multiple witnesses to the life of Jesus and the
early church. Second, the designation of four canonical Gospels undermines
the view that the Divine can be contained in a book. Bibliolatry, the worship
of the Bible, is rejected. The Gospels witness to the life of Jesus, they are not
identical to Jesus. (See a Christian response to question five) Third, diversity
of interpretation is built into the New Testament canon. The inconsistencies
in the Gospel accounts may frustrate the Christian who seeks "historical
proof," but, more important, it invites freedom of inquiry and reinterpretation.
Finally, numerous Gospels complement each other. The four canonical
Gospels and the extracanonical Gospels broaden our understanding of the
"diversity and complexity of the early Jesus traditions." Because multiple
contexts and voices are preserved, our knowledge and appreciation of the
early church is expanded and enriched.

Although no sacred or single reason grounds the church's decision to canonize four Gospels, that number gained prominence by the end of the second century and was finalized by the fourth century.

Question Four: Is there a Difference Between Faith and Belief?

As mentioned in chapter one, Christians currently use the words *faith* and *belief* interchangeably. For example, "do you *believe* in God?" means the same as "do you have *faith* in God?" Although the Christian Bridge-Link is Faith-Belief (see chapter two, "The Christian Structure"), the use of these words as synonyms is modern.

Prior to the Protestant Reformation, these words were not equivalent. For the first sixteen centuries of the Christian tradition, *faith* meant "trust of the heart in God's freely promised mercy and grace." After the death in 1546 of Martin Luther, the German Protestant Reformer, the interpretation of his famous motto "justification by grace through faith" evolved into a more intellectualistic notion of *faith* as "assent" to particular articles of belief. Around the same time, William Shakespeare (1564–1616) was one of the last writers to use *faith*, which was once a verb in English, as a participle. Protestant Scholasticism, where *faith* meant "intellectual agreement," was born.

The trend to equate *faith* and *belief* was accelerated by the Enlightenment's challenge to the major tenets and teachings of the Christian tradition (see a Christian response to question nine). Placed in a defensive posture and preoccupied with preserving its central doctrines, both Roman Catholicism and Protestantism responded during the eighteenth and nineteenth centuries by strengthening their grip on "correct belief." As a result, modern western culture equates *faith* and *belief* as virtual synonyms.

Regrettably the identification of *faith* with *belief* diminished modern Christianity's ability to distinguish between the relational and the intellectual dimensions of a believer's confession of Jesus as the Christ. Over the past two centuries, *faith* became associated more and more with religious certainty — just the opposite of its original meaning. According to the Apostle Paul in the fifth chapter of the Letter to the Romans, Christians "hope for what we do not see" because "hope that is seen is not hope."

For the early church, *faith* occurred when people did not or could not know. *Faith* was, therefore, a "gamble" about what might be, not certainty about what was guaranteed. When *faith* is reduced to certainty, it is more about knowledge and less about a personal "wager."

Moreover, Christians have *faith* in a person (Jesus the Christ), not in any particular doctrine. The Apostle Paul in chapter three of Romans summaries the good news of the Gospel when he writes that people "are now justified by his grace as a gift, through the redemption that is in Christ Jesus . . . effective through faith."

Consequently, *faith* is a relational category whose equivalent is "trust." The Christian life is first and foremost about a person's relationship to the God who is revealed in the life, death, and resurrection of Jesus of Nazareth. Hence, *faith* refers to the positive response of a person who either hears God's redemptive Word or encounters God's redemptive acts in history.

Therefore, *faith* is a "first order" occurrence. An intimate relationship with another person is based on trust. One "knows" the other person in the sense that the other has self-disclosed a consistent pattern of behavior that elicits assurance. When we speak about having *faith* in a person, we really mean that we have confidence in the person to be dependable in thought and action. Since *faith* is a relational category, trust, not belief, is the proper synonym.

By contrast, *belief* is a "second order" occurrence. It refers to the intentional process of "making sense" of a prior event. To understand an experience means stepping back and detaching oneself from the encounter. It involves the cognitive process of reflecting upon the meaning and the message of that event.

Thus, the Christian first encounters or is encountered by the risen Lord (a dramatic example is the Apostle Paul's experience of Jesus on the road to Damascus as recorded in the book of Acts chapters 9, 22, and 26) and then proceeds to make sense of that event. If that moment of revelation elicits trust, then *faith* is present. Only later does the Christian interpret the significance of that encounter in terms of what he believes it means for his life.

This individual process of response and reflection also occurs on a collective level. As the church's intentional reflection on the language and practice of faith, theology ("words about God") is a "second-order" event. What the community understands about God and Jesus is proclaimed, preserved, and transmitted in the various church creeds. Not surprisingly, the root meaning of the word "creed" comes from the Latin *credo* which means "to believe."

Thus the answer to the above question is that there is a major difference in the traditional Christian meaning of the words *faith* and *belief*. The former refers to a "first order" experience of another person, while the latter refers to the "second order" subsequent effort to make sense of that experience. The recovery of these separate meanings of *faith* and *belief* would greatly enhance the church's ability to both interpret and articulate two distinct but interrelated dynamics of the Christian life. However, for the purposes of our book we have retained the commonplace use of the words as synonyms.

Question Five: Is the Bible (both Old and New Testaments) the Word of God for Christians?

This question is deceptively complex. On the one hand, the Christian tradition has always affirmed the Bible (both Old and New Testaments) as the "Word of God." Thus, the initial and instinctive answer to this question is an unambiguous "yes." On the other hand, the Christian tradition has also affirmed Jesus as the "Word of God." This preeminent claim qualifies the first response.

In order to understand these two apparently contradictory Christian claims, we need to explore the interrelationship between God, Christ, Word of God, and Bible. For the Abrahamic traditions (Judaism, Christianity, and Islam), the term "God" ("Allah") is the name that references the "ultimate mystery" that grounds all of life yet also transcends it. Most important, God can be "known" (although neither exhausted nor fully comprehended), because God reveals who God is in history. The act of God's self-disclosure in time and space is called "revelation."

Each of the Abrahamic traditions has designated a single act in history as the normative revelation of God by which all other revelations are evaluated. For Judaism, the decisive revelation is the dual event of the exodus of the Hebrew slaves (later the Jewish People) from Egypt and the subsequent giving of the Ten Commandments by God to Moses on Mount Sinai. These two events establish the covenant between God and the Jewish people (see chapter two, "The Jewish Structure"). For Islam, the constitutive event is the revelation of the Koran to Mohammad. For Christianity, the definitive revelation of God in history is the crucifixion and resurrection of Jesus of Nazareth.

Unique to Christianity, the "Word of God" is not a book (Hebrew Bible or Koran) but a person—Jesus the Christ. The ultimate authority for the church is the crucified, resurrected, and living Lord. (This is a theological statement of Faith-Belief that affirms Christ as the Essential Element for Christianity.) That assertion distinguishes Christianity from the other two Abrahamic traditions. The prologue to the Gospel of John underscores this Christian affirmation: "In the beginning was the Word, and the Word was with God, and the Word was God . . . And the Word became flesh and lived among us . . . The law indeed was given through Moses; grace and truth came through Jesus Christ. No one has ever seen God. It is God the only Son, who is close to the Father's heart, who has made him known" (selections from John 1:1–18).

Yet a paradox exists. On the one hand, the historical Jesus of Nazareth is dead. Because crucifixion means the physical death of Jesus, denial of this "historical fact" undermines the humanity of Jesus. As a result, present-day Christians cannot "know" Jesus face-to-face like they "know" other people in their lives. Therefore, the New Testament is important since it contains the primary witness of the early church to the life and teachings of Jesus who is professed the Christ. Without the Gospels, Christians would not have historical access to the person Jesus—his message and meaning.

On the other hand, Christians claim that the historical Jesus is resurrected from the dead (see a Christian response to question one). Not only is the "Word of God" a person and not a book, but the "Word of God" is living Lord. That is, Jesus is living and not dead. Consequently, the Christian norm is Jesus Christ, "the same yesterday and today and forever" (Hebrews 13:8)

We are now ready to answer the question: Is the Bible (both Old and New Testaments) the Word of God for Christians? Based upon the preceding explanation, the answer is *both* "no" and "yes"—in that order! It is "no," because for Christianity Jesus Christ, the crucified, risen, and living Lord, is the ultimate authority for the church. As testified by the Gospel of John, Jesus is the "Word of God" incarnate.

The answer is "yes," since the Bible (both Old and New Testaments) is the "Word of God" in a secondary sense. Because the Christian Bible narrates the primary witness to both the Jewish and Christian normative revelations of God in history (the Christian scriptures contain two testaments—Old Testament and New Testament—see a Christian response to question six), it occupies an inordinately important role in the Christian tradition. The Bible "contains" the "Word of God," but it is not identical to the Word. That is, the Bible for Christians derives its authority from its primary witness to Jesus. However, it should never be mistaken for the Word itself. People never equate a biography of a person, regardless of its quality or thoroughness, with the person. Elevation of any book to that status would diminish the person. More important, the Christian tradition does not want to domesticate God by claiming that the "ultimate mystery" of life, in this case the normative revelation of the "Word of God" incarnate, is reducible to a book. The identification of the content (God or Jesus) with the vehicle (Bible) commits the heresy of Bibliolatry (worship of the book).

To summarize, Jesus as living Lord is first and foremost the "Word of God" for Christians. The Bible (both Old and New Testaments) can also be referred to as the "Word of God" but only in a secondary sense. As the historical witness to God's self-disclosure in Jesus, the Bible derives its authority from the person it portrays.

Question Six: Why Do Christians Call the Hebrew Bible the Old Testament?

This is an exceedingly important question because it revisits the critical issue of the Christian attitude toward Judaism. The legacy of Israel is especially significant for the origins of Christianity, as well as for the myth of "Judaism is Christianity without Christ" that we described and refuted in chapter one.

From its inception, Christianity has interpreted the Hebrew Bible as foretelling the coming of the Messiah and has quoted from it to "prove" that Jesus is the Christ. In response, therefore, to a proposal in the 140s by Marcion, a wealthy member of the Christian community in Rome, to reject the entire "Old Testament," the church affirmed the continuity between Judaism and Christianity by deciding to include the Jewish canon in the Christian Bible. Thus, the interrelationship between Judaism and Christianity became inescapable and intentional. This unprecedented inclusion permanently links the Christian community to the Jewish people of Biblical times. Hence, this response will address three concerns: the derivation and meaning of the term "Old Testament," the debate over the term and alternative designations, and the reason for the different order of the books of the "Old Testament" for Judaism and the various branches of Christianity.

The term "Old Testament" is the Christian name for the first section of the Christian Bible that is (for the most part) identical in content but not in order to the Scriptures of ancient Israel. Although these books are not the only writings in the Christian canon, they are the works that are "common" to both religions.

According to Christian tradition, the distinction between "Old Testament" and "New Testament" is based on a passage from the prophet Jeremiah:

> The days are surely coming, says the Lord, when I will make a new covenant with the house of Israel and the house of Judah. It will not be like the covenant that I made with their ancestors when I took them by the hand to bring them out of the land of Egypt—a covenant that they broke, though I was their husband, says the Lord. But this is the covenant that I will make with the house of Israel after those days, says the Lord . . . (31:31–33).

The English word "testament" comes from the Latin translation of the Greek *diatheke* which can mean either "testament" or "covenant." While early Christian writers alluded to an old and a new covenant (II Corinthians 3:14 and Hebrews 8:7), it was Tertullian (160–230), the first major theologian to write in Latin, and Origen (185–254), one of the most influential Greek-speaking theologians, who first used the term "Old Testament" to describe the Jewish books of the Christian Bible.

In recent years, scholars of the Bible and comparative religions have begun to question the appropriateness of this traditional Christian term. Four concerns have surfaced. First, the word "old" has a pejorative connotation for most moderns. Linking this word to the Jewish Scriptures might suggest, then, that these writings are "no longer useful" and should be replaced by a

more valuable or "new" set of writings. Consequently, the label "old" undermines both the autonomy and integrity of the Hebrew texts. Second, the word
"testament" is often associated with a person's "last will and testament." Because of this relationship to "death," an "old testament" seems doubly in need
of something "new." Third, the connection of the Jewish Bible to the terms
"old" and "testament" runs the risk, for Christians, of losing the "living
sense" of these writings. If the "Old Testament" functions as an extended prologue to the "New Testament" at best and a "testament to a dead religion" at
worst, then the Christian reader never values the books of the Hebrew Bible
as vital to the corporate life of a living religious tradition. Fourth, and most
important, the term "Old Testament" is tainted with the supersessionist
agenda that, in the name of Jesus, the Jews are rejected by God and replaced
by the Christians.

For these reasons, scholars have tried to identify alternative terms that can
both address the above concerns and preserve the continuity between the God
of Abraham and the God of Jesus. Substitute titles include: Hebrew and Greek
Scriptures, Jewish and Christian Scriptures, and First and Second Testaments.
Unfortunately, none of these suggestions is satisfactory. The terms "Hebrew"
and "Jewish" could imply that Christians "ceded" these books back to the
Jews, thereby echoing Marcion and endorsing discontinuity. Furthermore, not
all the books included in the Roman Catholic canon are written in Hebrew
(for example, Wisdom of Solomon and 2 Maccabees are in Greek). In addition, the use of "first" and "second" does not avoid the earlier complaint
about "old" and "new." Because Christianity cannot be understood apart from
Judaism and its Scriptures, the terms that Christians use to identify the Hebrew Bible are very important. However, no consensus exists on this topic in
the present or for the foreseeable future.

The interrelationship between Judaism and Christianity is not only affected
by the names that we use to designate Scripture but also by the arrangement
of the books in the "Old Testament." For the Jewish community, the Hebrew
Bible is divided into three major sections: Torah or Pentateuch (the Five
Books of Moses: Genesis, Exodus, Leviticus, Numbers, Deuteronomy), the
Prophets (Joshua, Judges, 1–2 Samuel, and 1–2 Kings comprise the Former
Prophets, while Isaiah, Jeremiah, Ezekiel, and the twelve Minor Prophets
comprise the Latter Prophets), and the Writings (Psalms, Job, Proverbs, Ruth,
Song of Songs, Ecclesiastes, Lamentations, Esther, Daniel, Ezra-Nehemiah,
1–2 Chronicles). These 24 books are frequently called "Tanak," an acronym
derived from the first Hebrew letter of the name for each major division.

After the first five books of the Torah, the Christian "Old Testament" varies
not only in order but also, in some cases, in content. These differences can be
explained by the history of the Bible in the two religious communities. The

Jewish Bible, with the exception of a few chapters in Aramaic, was written in Hebrew. During the Hellenistic period (325–63 B.C.E.), various Jewish communities outside of Palestine (Diaspora Judaism), especially in Alexandria, Egypt, translated these books into Greek. It was the Alexandrian Greek version of the Hebrew Bible, the Septuagint, that became the "Old Testament" for the Greek-speaking Christian community.

The Christian Bible follows the same order as the Hebrew Bible from Genesis to 1–2 Kings with the one exception of the insertion of Ruth after Judges. Then the *main difference* occurs. In the Jewish tradition, the historical section is immediately followed by the literary Prophets and then by the Writings (the last two sections of the Tanak). In the Christian tradition, however, the order of these sections is reversed. The Writings come after the historical section (1–2 Kings, 1–2 Chronicles, Ezra and Nehemiah, and Esther) and the Prophets, including the Book of Daniel, complete the Christian "Old Testament." Malachi, the last book of the twelve Minor Prophets, leads directly into the Gospels in the Protestant canon. The significance of this change in order cannot be understated. "For Christians," according to David Noel Freedman, an esteemed Biblical scholar, "the Old Testament is a book of prophecy and prediction of the coming of the Messiah that is fulfilled in the New Testament." This theological conviction determines the Christian arrangement of the books.

Although the Christian "Old Testament" includes the same books as the Hebrew Bible, the numbering is also different. For Protestants, the Hebrew Bible includes 39, not 24, books. This difference is easily explained. The "two-volume" historical books (1–2 Samuel, 1–2 Kings, 1–2 Chronicles, Ezra-Nehemiah) and the twelve Minor Prophets are counted as separate books in the Protestant "Old Testament." For Roman Catholics, however, there are 46 books in the "Old Testament." In addition to the 39 books, there are 7 other books (1–2 Maccabees, Judith, Tobit, Baruch, Sirach and the Wisdom of Solomon). These texts were a part of the Greek Septuagint but not included in the original Hebrew Bible or accepted as part of the historic Jewish canon. For the early Christian community, the common book of Scripture was the Septuagint. Consequently, scholars sometimes refer to this collection of 46 books as the "Alexandrian canon" as opposed to the smaller "Palestinian (Jewish) canon."

For Orthodox Christians, the count is higher. The Greek Orthodox Church adds 3 Maccabees and 2 Esdras to the Roman Catholic canon, while the Ethiopian Orthodox Church includes I Enoch, Jubilees, and more. The Protestant Reformers of the sixteenth century made the last change to the number of books in the "Old Testament." Invoking the principle of *sola scriptura* (Scripture alone), they retrieved what they believed was the earlier, and shorter, form of the Hebrew Bible and therefore removed the 7 additional books of the Roman Catholic "Old Testament." Protestants refer to these books as the "Apocrypha" ("hidden" books) and often place them between the "Old Testament" and "New Testament" in their current Bible publications.

In conclusion, regardless of the terms Christians use to designate the Hebrew Bible, or the arrangement and number of the books, all Christian communities incorporate these writings into their canon. This inclusion testifies to the deliberate intention of all churches to preserve the historic connection between these two religious traditions.

Question Seven: How Do Christians Interpret the Hebrew Bible?

From its inception, Christianity has "laid claim" to the Hebrew Bible as its own. In the second century C.E., the church dismissed Marcion's radical proposal to discard the Old Testament on the grounds that the Hebrew Bible witnessed to Christ. The nascent Christian movement interpreted the Old Testament in light of the conviction that the Jewish prophecy of the Messiah was fulfilled in Jesus of Nazareth.

This response will provide an overview of the Christian interpretation of the Old Testament in four time periods: the early church, the Middle Ages, the Reformation, and the modern era.[2]

The early Christian community assumed that the Old Testament belonged to them and that its authority derived from the text's relationship to Christ. Although the church did not systematically define theories of Biblical interpretation, scholars traditionally identify three separate but overlapping methods of interpretation: prophecy, allegory, and typology.

The practice of interpreting the Old Testament as "predicting" something that would happen in the future—usually related to Jesus but also to the time of the reader—is probably the most familiar method to us today. Based on the misunderstanding that a Biblical prophet is someone who "foretells the future," rather than someone who "speaks in the name of God," this method of "prooftexting" is found throughout the New Testament. The best examples are found in the Gospel of Matthew where the theme of prophecy fulfilled is tied to the birth of Jesus (Matthew 1:22–23 invokes Isaiah 7:14), the place of Jesus' birth (Matthew 2:5–6 combines Micah 5:2 and 2 Samuel 5:2), the flight to Egypt (Matthew 2:15 recalls Hosea 11:1), the slaughter of the innocents (Matthew 2:17–18 cites Jeremiah 31:15), the decision to settle in Nazareth (Matthew 2:23 alludes to numerous Old Testament passages), as well as other events in the life of Jesus.

Prophecy fulfillment was popular both then and now because it is a "fairly simple and straightforward method" of demonstrating the continuity between the two religions. However, this strength also pinpoints its weakness—most

Old Testament texts neither mention nor relate in any way to the coming Messiah. Therefore, the prophecy method does not apply to the vast majority of the Hebrew Bible. Even when it does apply, the implication is that the meaning of the passage only relates to the time of the interpreter and not to the time of the prophet and the intervening generation of readers.

Because of these limitations of the prophecy fulfillment method, Christians borrowed the allegorical method from the Greeks and Jews. One obvious advantage of this method was its ability to find "spiritual" meaning in narratives that first appeared crass and objectionable. A leading proponent of allegory, Origen of Alexandria (185–254), advocated a hierarchical triple method of Biblical interpretation (literal, moral, and spiritual meanings) that paralleled the tripartite constitution of the human (body, soul, and spirit). Since the entire Bible for Origen was an allegorical document, the reader must discover the hidden meaning behind the surface words that is couched in allegory.

This method was especially helpful in interpreting controversial narratives like the Genesis creation story. Origen wrote:

> For who that has understanding will suppose that the first, and second, and third day, and the evening and the morning, existed without a sun, a moon, and stars? . . . And who is so foolish as to suppose that God . . . planted a paradise in Eden . . . and again, that one was a partaker of good and evil by masticating what was taken from a tree? And if God is said to walk in the paradise in the evening, and Adam to hide himself under a tree, I do not suppose that any one doubts that these things figuratively indicate certain mysteries, the history having taken place in appearance and not literally.[3]

Although the advantage of allegory over prophecy was that it can be applied to any and all Biblical texts, its fundamental flaw was that it made "the interpreter master of the text and its meaning, rather than vice versa." Furthermore, allegory concentrated on the meaning of words and neglected the narrative event. Thus, prophecy, preoccupied with the fulfillment of a predication in a future event, interpreted the words literally, while allegory, preoccupied with eternal and moral truths, interpreted the words metaphorically.

Like prophecy, typology (the third method) focused on a future event, but, unlike prophecy, typology valued the past event since it participated in God's guidance of history toward its goal. For Christians, the life, death, and resurrection of Jesus was the telos of history. All events from the beginning of time are ordained by God to point to Christ. Thus, Irenaeus, Bishop of Lyons in the late second century, wrote: "It is not by means of visions alone which were seen, and words which were proclaimed, but also in actual works, that (Jesus) was beheld by the prophets, in order that through them He might prefigure and show forth future events beforehand."[4]

Although all three methods of Biblical interpretation were employed by early Christian expositors of Scripture, typology was the most common. Justin Martyr, a noted Christian apologist of the second century, provided a typical example: "The mystery, then, of the lamb which God enjoined to be sacrificed as the Passover, was a type of Christ; with whose blood, in proportion to their faith in Him, they anoint their houses, i.e., themselves, who believe in Him."[5]

During the Middle Ages, the maxim—"there is no meaning without context"—was most applicable. Two Christian settings influenced Biblical interpretation: medieval monasticism, and cathedral schools and medieval universities. A monastic reading of the Scriptures highlighted two interests. First, the Bible was "usually interpreted as a call to monastic renunciation and contemplation" and, therefore, read allegorically. The stories of Moses, Job, and Ezekiel, as well as the Song of Songs, were understood as a metaphor for the soul's ascent to God and the avoidance of the perils along the way. Second, the Bible was read and sung in the context of prayer and worship. Hence, Psalm 51 was heard on Ash Wednesday (the first day of the Christian season of Lent), Isaiah 53 was heard on Good Friday (the day of Christ's crucifixion), and Isaiah 9 and 11 were heard during Advent (the season prior to Christmas).

Because the overarching goal of reading Scripture for the monk was the love of God, and not knowledge, the Old Testament was frequently read to find Christ. Thus, Bernard of Clairvaux, the great mystic of the twelfth century, could insist: "I no longer wish to listen to Moses, whom I find to be no more than a stutterer. Isaiah's lips are unclean. Jeremiah cannot speak, for he is but a child. Actually, all the prophets are mutes. Let me rather listen to Him of whom they speak."[6]

For the Biblical interpreter of cathedral schools, and later in the universities, Scripture was read "as a source of knowledge and as a means of settling intellectual disagreements and disputes." Hence, the Bible was the "great arbiter" and the vehicle for "prooftexting." Neither extended interpretations nor moral exhortations were desired. Short passages or single verses were employed to "prove a point." Although the production of Biblical commentaries began in cathedral schools, and theologians like Thomas Aquinas developed the "scholastic method," Biblical interpretation was more often than not a means to an end.

Yet the medieval fixation on "prooftexting" spawned a growing interest in Biblical languages, as well as the customs and traditions of ancient Israel. Wherever possible, particularly in Spain where Jews, Christians, and Muslims co-existed, Christian scholars sought the guidance of rabbis.

With the advent of the Protestant Reformation and the slogan *sola scriptura* (scripture alone) in the sixteenth century, Biblical interpretation became more paramount. Yet new methods were not created. Schooled in the old ways, Reformers like Martin Luther and John Calvin appropriated selectively. As an Augustinian monk, Luther appreciated the medieval monastic tradition. As a professor of Bible, he valued scholarship and philology (study of words). As a Reformer, Luther read Scripture as a source for doctrine and debate. Most often, he interpreted the Bible either typologically or allegorically. As a humanist, Calvin insisted on learning the historical context of the passage. As a lawyer, he applied the "principle of accommodation," where God's revelation in Scripture was adjusted to suit the human context. Because subsequent generations of Protestant Biblical interpreters placed greater and greater emphasis on the Scriptures as "inspired" and "inerrant," literalism became more common.

Christian treatments of the Old Testament in the modern era are diverse in both their methods and interpretations. All of the previously mentioned Biblical methods are employed, as well as a significant new one—the historical-critical method. Most important, this approach "levels" the Old and New Testaments by insisting on a reading that values the text more than the opinions of the interpreters. According to the historical-critical method, an open examination of the sacred writings requires two presuppositions: (1) the Bible, as a collection of documents written by humans, is subject to the same investigation as any other literary work and (2) the text must first be understood in its original historical and cultural context, and only then seek its relevance for today. These principles affirm the autonomy, authority, and authenticity of the Hebrew Bible on its own terms. Regardless of the specific method applied (textual or literary, cross-cultural or gender), Christians who employ the precepts of the historical-critical method read, to the best of their ability, the Jewish text first and foremost in its historical and religious context.

In conclusion, the Christian convictions that guided the reading of the Old Testament during the first three periods that we have described still apply today. Consequently, neither a consensus method nor a consistent approach characterizes either the individual Christian's or a particular church's reading of the Hebrew Bible. Like the world around us, diversity reigns—including how Christians interpret the Old Testament today.

Question Eight: What is the Difference Between Roman Catholicism and Protestantism?

This question addresses the feature of our Structure that we call "Rays" as presented in chapter two. The Rays are the "vehicles of inclusion" by which a person participates in his Religion in order to be recognized as a member of that specific tradition. In Christianity, an individual proceeds through the

Structure by professing his belief (the Bridge-Link) that Jesus is the Christ (the Essential Element) and only then selects a specific church or denomination. The Rays above the Christian Structure identify these options—the diversity of denominations.

According to the *World Christian Encyclopedia*,[7] more than five billion people, or 85% of the world's population, affiliate with one of the world's 10,000 distinct religions. By far the single largest religion is Christianity, with more than two billion adherents, or 33% of the world's population. In America, there are 225 million Christians, or 85% of the population. (By way of comparison, less than one percent of the world's population is Jewish—14.5 million—and there are 5.6 million American Jews.) However, Christianity is fragmented into over 34,000 different denominations. This makes the task of describing the differences within Christianity exceedingly complex, and thus this response can provide only general observations.

Church historians divide modern Christianity into three broad categories that resulted from the two major schisms within the church.[8] The first split, which is traditionally dated to 1054, divided the Latin-speaking western churches (what we now call "Roman Catholicism") from the Greek-speaking eastern churches (what we now call the "Orthodox" or the "Eastern Orthodox Church"). The second split occurred with the European Reformation of the sixteenth century. It separated Roman Catholicism into two distinct groups; Catholics and Protestants. Protestantism almost immediately and permanently subdivided itself into internal divisions usually called "denominations."

Although the initial question only identifies two of the three branches of Christendom, this response will broaden its focus to include all three major divisions. The description of each branch will include its historical context, demographic information, and general characteristics.

ROMAN CATHOLICISM

Roman Catholicism (also called "Catholicism") is by far the largest form of Christianity in the world today. There are more than one billion Catholics worldwide, one-half of all Christians. Although originally identified with western and central Europe, Catholicism spread with the colonial expansion of Spain, Portugal, and France in the sixteenth century and Belgium in the nineteenth century to North and South America, as well as Africa, the Philippines, and India.

Traditionally the Roman Catholic Church has understood itself to be the "True Church." Citing Matthew 16:18 ("And I tell you, you are Peter, and on this rock I will build my church, and the gates of Hades will not prevail against it."), Catholics believe that Jesus appointed Peter as head of the church before He ascended into Heaven. Therefore, it is the "True Church" because it alone possesses the four marks of the "True Church of Christ": one, holy, catholic, and apostolic.

The Roman Catholic Church is *one* because it believes that there is only one Christian Church that is united in faith, in worship, and in succession from the Apostles of the early church. The Dogmatic Constitution on the Church, the seminal document of the Second Vatican Council (1962–1965), states: "The sole Church of Christ [is that] which our Saviour, after His Resurrection, entrusted to Peter's pastoral care, commissioning him and the other apostles to extend and rule it . . . This Church, constituted and organized as a society in the present world, subsists in the Catholic Church, which is governed by the successor of Peter and by the bishops in communion with him." According to the 1994 *Catechism of the Catholic Church*, "The Church is one: she acknowledges one Lord, confesses one faith, is born of one Baptism, forms only one Body, is given life by one Spirit, for the sake of one hope, at whose fulfillment all divisions will be overcome." In spite of the scandals of division, the Catholic Church is still one since "all those separated from the Catholic Church remain part of her, in a mysterious way."

The Roman Catholic Church is *holy* because Christ loves the Church as "his Bride, giving himself up for her so as to sanctify her." The paradox is that the Church is holy and perfect yet composed of imperfect and sinful people. The *Catechism of the Catholic Church* explains this mystery: "The Church is holy . . . Since she still includes sinners, she is 'the sinless one made up of sinners.' Her holiness shines in the saints; in Mary she is already all-holy."

The Roman Catholic Church is *catholic* in the sense that "lower case 'c' catholic" means "universal." The Church literally covers the earth from Saint Peter's Basilica in Rome, Italy, to the Amazon, to South Africa. Because all of these churches are in communion with each other and with the Bishop of Rome, the Catholic Church is truly universal. According to the *Catechism of the Catholic Church*, the Church "bears in herself and administers the totality of the means of salvation. She is sent out to all peoples. She speaks to all men. She encompasses all times."

The Roman Catholic Church is *apostolic* because of the concept of "apostolic succession." All Catholic bishops trace their ordination back to the Apostles of the early church as guided by the Holy Spirit who descended on the Apostles at Pentecost (Acts 2). Although other churches who are not in communion with the Church of Rome (like the Orthodox or Anglican Churches) also claim Apostolic succession, the Catholic Church enjoys historical priority. The new Catechism states: "The Church is apostolic. She is built on a lasting foundation: 'the twelve apostles of the Lamb.' She is indestructible. She is upheld infallibly in the truth; Christ governs her through Peter and the other apostles, who are present in their successors, the Pope and the college of bishops."

Although a church of one billion adherents and two thousand years of history defies simple generalizations, eight characteristics distinguish Roman Catholicism from the other forms of Christianity. First, the Roman Catholic Church is very hierarchical in governance. The Pope (the vicar of Christ on earth, also the Bishop of Rome) has considerable influence over the appointment of cardinals and bishops (church administrative and pastoral leaders) throughout the Catholic world, as well as over Biblical, theological, and ethical interpretations for all Catholics. After the death of a pope, the College of Cardinals meets in secret sessions to elect a successor.

Second, the city of Rome has particular significance in the Catholic world. As the name implies, "Roman" Catholicism identifies the Italian city of Rome as the "spiritual epicenter" of Catholicism. Beginning with its inception during the Roman Empire, the pope has most often resided in Rome and since 1929 the 108 acres of Vatican City have been the official residence of the pope and the administrative center of Catholicism. Pilgrimages are frequently made to Rome to see not only the pope (who holds an "audience" with people every Wednesday) but also the historic sites associated with the apostles Peter and Paul who are believed to have been martyred and buried in Rome.

Third, the Roman Catholic Church understands itself to be a "visible divine institution, whose structures are grounded in divine reality." Although the Second Vatican Council modified earlier absolutist claims, the Catholic Church still embodies the four marks of the True Church, as previously discussed. Therefore, its sense of teaching authority is top down. The *magisterium*, or teaching office of the church, plays a prominent role in the life of Catholics since no one is free to interpret Scripture "contrary to the sense in which Holy Mother Church, who is to judge the true sense and interpretation of the Holy Scriptures, has held and does hold."

Fourth, priests play an influential role in the Catholic life because of the hierarchical nature of the Roman Catholic Church. Most significant for today, as well as a key difference between the other two major divisions, Catholic clergy are exclusively male and not permitted to marry.

Fifth, Catholicism is a distinctly liturgical community of faith. Because the liturgy (literally "the work of the people," this term refers to the order of the worship service) is understood as a "public statement of the beliefs and values of the church, and a means by which continuity with the apostolic tradition" is preserved, the forms of worship are fixed and found in a prayer book. Although the Second Vatican Council replaced Latin with the vernacular tongue in local worship, the structure of the service remained uniform.

Sixth, Catholicism is also strongly sacramental. Believing that the benefits of Christ that resulted from his death and resurrection are available to communicants through the church's administration of the sacraments (rituals of the church that constitute a "visible form of invisible grace"), Roman Catholicism recognizes seven sacraments (Protestants acknowledge only two). They are: Baptism, Confirmation, Eucharist, Penance and Reconciliation, Anointing of the Sick, Holy Orders (Ordination), and Matrimony. The central sacrament is the Eucharist (also referred to as the Mass or Lord's Supper) which makes available to the church in each celebration "the real presence" of Christ, or the saving grace of the body and blood of Christ.

Seventh, monasticism continues to play an important role in shaping the Catholic ethos. Although there has been a recent decline in the traditional religious orders for both men and women, they nevertheless play a major role in the spiritual formation of lay Christians—both Catholic and Protestant. Spiritual retreats at Catholic centers are common for many Christian communities.

Eighth, but by no means least, the Catholic emphasis on the role of the saints in general and the Virgin Mary (the mother of Jesus, see especially Luke 1:39–56) in particular distinguishes the Roman Catholic Church from other forms of Christianity. Since the saints and Mary lived exemplary lives, they can serve as intercessors to God and Christ for both the living and the dead. The doctrine of the immaculate conception of Mary asserts that she was conceived without the contamination of original sin which justifies her adoration as the mother of Jesus (see a Christian response to question two). Catholic scholars differentiate between the *veneration* due to Mary and the *worship* which is due to God and Christ alone.

THE ORTHODOX CHURCH

We now turn to an examination of the Orthodox Church which numbers 216 million adherents today (or one in every ten Christians) and is strongest numerically in eastern Europe, particularly in Russia and Greece. Both the name and the tradition are generally unfamiliar to many North Americans. The term "Orthodox," when capitalized, refers to Orthodox Christians. Sometimes this branch of Christianity is called the "Eastern Orthodox Church." Historically this form of Christianity—Greek, Russian or Armenian Orthodox—retains continuity with the early Greek-speaking church of the east and traces its liturgy and doctrines back to that early church. When "orthodox" is not capitalized, the word usually means "correct or right" thought. For example, a study of "orthodox Christian beliefs" usually refers to beliefs held in common by a broad range of Christians through the centuries.

Since one of the initial tasks of the early church was to define its theological boundaries, debates frequently occurred over the language and meaning of the church's beliefs. These disputes centered on how Jesus could be both divine and human, and the Trinity (see a Christian response to question ten). Church councils were called to resolve these conflicts by providing the bedrock formulations for the centuries. The ongoing search for "orthodox" Christianity from 325 C.E. (Constantine solidified the empire, "the cause of Rome and Christ are one," and the first ecumenical council at Nicaea is called) to 800 (the seventh and final ecumenical council concludes) both describes the ethos and names this branch of Christendom.

By the fourth century of the Common Era, there were five major centers of Christianity: Rome, Constantinople (new Rome), Alexandria, Antioch, and Jerusalem. Churches of the east acknowledged the equality of the patriarchs from these cities, while churches of the west acknowledged the superiority of the patriarch of Rome. Although the technical split between the east and the west is dated to 1054 when the Pope and the Patriarch of Constantinople excommunicated each other, the schism evolved over the preceding centuries. During the fourth century, Constantine moved the capital from Rome to Byzantium, and renamed it Constantinople. By the fifth century many theologians in the west could scarcely read Greek, while Christians in the east paid little attention to Latin theology. Two major issues exposed the cultural gap between the eastern and western manifestations of the church.

The first issue revolved around the papacy. In the west, the Bishop of Rome was the sole leader of the church, while in the east leadership included the patriarchs of the five major cities and final authority resided with the church councils.

The second issue was theological. In the east, the Nicene Creed, formulated at the Council of Nicaea (now the city of Iznik in modern-day Turkey) in 325, constituted the central orthodox statement of the church. Yet in the west the Synod in Toledo, Spain, in 589 added the word *filioque* ("and the Son") to the creed. By 800, westerners recited the creed with the addition: "the Holy Spirit proceeds from the Father 'and the Son.'" This attachment infuriated the eastern church for two reasons. First and foremost, it tampered with the "inviolable" creed. Second, it denied the basis of unity for the Trinity in the Father and subordinated the Spirit to the Son. Neither a compromise nor a resolution was reached.

Other differences gradually surfaced. The west thought in terms of states: Adam fell into the state of sin and Christ redeemed humanity into the state of grace (therefore, there is no place for human work). The east thought in terms of processes: Christians move toward deification and consequently human works play a necessary role. At the Eucharist, the east used leavened bread, while the west used unleavened bread. The moment when the bread and the wine became the body and blood of Christ for the east was the epiclesis (Spirit descends) and for the west it was the recitation of the Words of Institution (Jesus' words at the Last Supper, see I Corinthians 11:23–26). In the east priests could marry, while in the west they could not.

Although the official split between the eastern and western branches of Christendom occurred in 1054, the irreparable break occurred in 1204 when the western Crusaders ransacked Constantinople. From that moment forward, the eastern church viewed the western church as the enemy. When Constantinople fell to the Turks in 1453, Russia (Moscow is the third Rome) became the lone defender of the Orthodox Church until the Bolshevik Revolution in 1917.

The distinctive ethos of the Orthodox Church can be described by the following six general characteristics. First, Orthodoxy in all of its forms claims historical continuity with the early church. Although tradition is a "living entity" that meets the new challenges presented by each succeeding age, it remains essentially unchanged. Therefore, the writings of the "Greek fathers" and their liturgical forms are highly valued.

Second, Orthodoxy recognizes only seven ecumenical councils as authoritative, and does not accept the pronouncements of any council after the Second Council of Nicaea in 787. The seven councils are: the first ecumenical council at Nicaea in 325 that affirmed Jesus as one in essence (*homoousios*) with God; the second ecumenical council at Constantinople in 381 that professed God as three persons (Father, Son, and Spirit); the third ecumenical council at Ephesus in 431 that declared Jesus as complete God and complete human in one person, as well as Mary the *theotokos* ("God Bearer" since she gave birth to Jesus, both divine and human); the fourth ecumenical council at Chalcedon in 451 that asserted Jesus as two natures, human and divine, in one person; the fifth ecumenical council at Constantinople in 553 that confirmed the two natures of Jesus; the sixth ecumenical council at Constantinople in 680 that claimed both natures of Christ acted freely and are united "mystically" in one divine person; and the seventh ecumenical council at Nicaea in 787 that decided it was proper to venerate images (icons) of Christ but true worship is only for God. Although local councils continue to meet and address specific concerns, the judgments of these gatherings do not carry the same authority as the first seven councils.

Third, Orthodoxy insists that the Holy Spirit proceeds from the Father alone and that salvation involves "deification." That is, "God became human, in order that humans might become God." As this theological cita-tion suggests, there is a strong connection in the Orthodox Church between the doctrines of the incarnation (God became human in the person of Jesus) and soteriology (the understanding of salvation). For Orthodoxy, the divine did not merely assume the specific human person of Jesus, but also human nature in general. Consequently, humanity is able to share in the deification which results from the incarnation. Since humans are cre-ated to be in relationship to God, all humans have this possibility because of Jesus.

Fourth, only Orthodoxy uses icons (images) in their worship and spiritual life. These theologically specific pictures of Jesus, Mary, the apostles, and the saints serve as "windows of perception" through which believers may en-counter the divine reality.

Fifth, Orthodoxy, like Catholicism, values the monastic life. Perhaps the most important monastic center is Mount Athos, a peninsula that stretches into the Aegean Sea. Most Orthodox bishops come from monasteries.

Sixth, Orthodox clergy, unlike Catholic priests, are permitted to marry (be-fore ordination) but bishops are generally unmarried (since most are monks). Like Catholicism, only males can be ordained.

PROTESTANTISM

We now turn our attention to Protestantism, the third and newest branch of Christianity. Born during the turbulent years of the sixteenth century in Eu-rope, Protestantism demolished once and for all the ancient Catholic ideal of a single church with the pope as its visible head. Moreover, the impulses for reform—social, political, economic, and theological—spawned countless splinter movements. Within decades there were significant yet divergent Protestant communities in Germany, Scandinavia, Switzerland, France, Eng-land, and Scotland. This extraordinary propensity to fragment, almost expo-nentially, accounts for the 34,000 different denominations among the 426 million Protestants in the world today.

Although the term "Protestant" generally refers to those churches that trace their origins to the divisions of sixteenth century Europe, its derivation is quite specific. Subsequent to the decision of the second Diet of Speyer in Feb-ruary, 1529, to end the toleration of Lutheranism in Germany, six princes and fourteen cities protested the denial of religious freedom. Thus, the "protest" in question was against neither Rome nor Catholic theology. However, the term "Protestant" applies today to any form of western Christianity that does not accept the authority of the pope.

Because the origins of Protestantism are exceedingly complex, we shall briefly discuss the three leading reformers: Martin Luther (1483–1546), Ulrich (Huldrych) Zwingli (1484–1531), and John Calvin (1509–1564).

Most historians date the beginning of the Protestant Reformation to October 31, 1517, when Martin Luther posted his ninety-five theses on the castle church door at Wittenberg, Germany. This call for theological debate over the selling of indulgences (a form of penance) by John Tetzel ("as soon as the coin in the coffer rings, the soul from purgatory springs") climaxed a long spiritual journey for Luther. Obsessed with his inability to know with certainty that he was saved, Luther directed his enormous intellectual powers on the doctrine of justification—the question of how humans can enter into a right relationship with God. Starting with the conventional Catholic position that individual achievement can advance one's justification, Luther concluded that this understanding was "seriously deficient" because salvation is accomplished by grace alone, through faith, as taught by the Apostle Paul in the Letter to the Romans. The concept of indulgences (that you can influence your salvation by buying pieces of paper) vitiated salvation as a free gift from God. Luther's motto, "justification by grace through faith," became the theological cornerstone for Protestantism. A prolific writer and debater, Luther's ideas quickly spread through Europe on the wings of the Gutenberg press.

The Swiss reformer Ulrich Zwingli reached similar conclusions to Luther's, although he pursued a different path. Educated at Vienna and Basel, Zwingli was a Christian humanist. As pastor of the most influential Protestant church in Zurich, Zwingli preached reform against Catholic abuses and theology. Although a denomination does not bear his name, his theological insights permeate much of Protestantism, especially his belief that the Lord's Supper is a memorial (remembrance) of Christ's death.

John Calvin, the major reformer of the Protestant second generation, was born in France, studied civil law, had a conversion experience which led to his involvement with the reforming movements, and became head of the Reformation in Geneva, Switzerland. His monumental work, *Institutes of the Christian Religion*, was the most systematic defense of Reformed theology at the time and still serves as a benchmark for Protestant theology.

Although the Reformation movement on the continent was spearheaded by prominent theologians, that was not the case in England. The need of Henry VIII (reigned from 1509–1547) to have a male heir to the throne precipitated a series of events that replaced papal authority with the English national church. After the short reigns of Edward VI (1547–1553) and Mary (1553–1558), who tried to restore Catholicism through a reign of terror (over 300 executions earned her the nickname of "Bloody Mary"),

Queen Elizabeth (1558–1603) stabilized the Church of England (Anglican or Episcopal Church in America). Her vision of a Reformed Episcopal church grounded in both Calvinist theology and a high church liturgy (based on the *Book of Common Prayer* by Thomas Cranmer) flourishes today. The most notable change for clergy was the right of bishops and priests to marry.

In addition to these "traditional" reformers, there were countless others who took more radical positions. One group, known by their pejorative name "Anabaptists" ("rebaptizers"), rejected the Catholic, Lutheran, and Calvinist sacrament of infant baptism and practiced adult baptism. Convinced that the church must following the teachings of the New Testament in general and the Sermon on the Mount (Matthew 5–7) in particular, many Anabaptists advocated a separation of church and state. They would neither swear oaths of allegiance nor participate in the military. Although many were pacifists, some thought that the end of the world was near and that they should establish the Kingdom of God on earth by force if necessary. These diverse Anabaptists are the religious forebears of the Baptists, Congregationalists, Quakers, and Mennonites.

As indicated by our historical narrative, Protestantism is virtually impossible to describe or define. Most church historians identify no less than seven distinct Protestant classifications today. They are: Anglicans, Baptists, Lutherans, Methodists (a movement that broke from the Church of England and emphasized the need for personal holiness), Reformed (denominations influenced by Calvin, like the Presbyterians), Evangelicals (usually found as movements within existing denominations that stress the literal interpretation of the Bible, the saving death of Jesus on the cross, personal conversion, and evangelism), and Charismatics (this movement may either take the form of a trend within Protestantism or Catholicism, or it may be a charismatic denomination like the "Assemblies of God" that emphasizes the power and activity of the Holy Spirit and is known for "speaking in tongues" or glossolalia). (The question of the relationship of other movements like the Jehovah's Witnesses, the Latter-Day Saints, and the Christian Scientists to Protestantism is too complicated to address here.) Nonetheless, the following seven characteristics locate the central themes of Protestantism—easily the most diverse branch of Christianity.

First, Protestants reject the authority of popes (Roman Catholic) and patriarchs (Orthodox), as well as the reverence for and the intercession of the saints and the Virgin Mary. Although the monastic life is viewed with suspicion, many Protestants value contemplative disciplines. In addition, priestly celibacy and purgatory are repudiated.

Second, Protestants dismiss the medieval system of seven sacraments and affirm at most two sacraments or ordinances—baptism (both infant and adult baptism are practiced) and the Lord's Supper (with an immensely broad range of meaning). Yet some Protestant groups, like the Quakers, do not practice any rituals that would be considered sacramental.

Third, Protestants place a high priority on the Bible. In its extreme form, Protestants believe that "the Bible, the whole Bible, and nothing but the Bible, is the religion of Protestants." The concept of *sola scriptura* (Scripture alone) denies, on the one hand, the Catholic emphasis on tradition and the *magisterium* as well as the Orthodox emphasis on the seven ecumenical councils, and confirms, on the other hand, the Bible as the ultimate foundation and authority for the Christian life.

Fourth, Protestants value the individual interpretation of scripture. Although this precept contributes to the continued fragmentation of Protestantism, the freedom to interpret the Bible according to the dictates of one's conscience is a hallmark of this Christian branch.

Fifth, Protestants affirm Luther's doctrine of "justification by grace through faith." The concepts of *sola gratia* (grace alone) and *sola fide* (faith alone) inform virtually all Protestant doctrines of salvation. Sinners are justified before God solely on the ground of Christ's sacrificial death on the cross and not by any human effort. Thus, grace is a divine gift that is appropriated through faith, not works.

Sixth, Protestants espouse the doctrine of the "priesthood of all believers." Luther rejected the medieval Catholic distinction between priests and laity, and replaced it with the notion that all baptized believers are priests to each other. "A Christian is a perfectly free lord of all, subject to none. A Christian is a perfectly dutiful servant of all, subject to all." Every believer is a priest in the sense that he can have direct access to the forgiving grace of God through Christ without the need of a mediator.

Seventh, Protestants preserve a healthy suspicion of institutions and individuals. Although this "Protestant Principle" contributes to conflict and division, it is grounded in Luther's Augustinian training. According to *The City of God*, Augustine's seminal response to Roman criticism of Christianity at the beginning of the fifth century, history has the possibility of both grandeur and corruption. Because humans are sinners, the danger of mistaking a finite object for the infinite is always present. The ambiguity of the human life requires, therefore, constant diligence.

In conclusion, the complexity and diversity of Christianity has necessitated a lengthy yet general response. The reader should now realize that the Rays above the Christian Structure represent an almost unimaginable number of denominational or church options through which the individual can participate in the Christian life.

Question Nine: Why are there so Many Protestant Denominations?

As mentioned in the previous response, the *World Christian Encyclopedia*[9] lists over 34,000 Protestant denominations in the world today. This staggering number seems to suggest that there are as many reasons for fragmentation as there are Protestants! Yet four general categories of explanation can be identified. They are: political, economic, theological, and cultural. Religion is inextricably woven into the fabric of human life.

The political is reflected in two examples from the era of the Protestant Reformation. The most obvious illustration of politics dividing the church was the creation of the Church of England. In 1509 Henry VIII married Catherine of Aragon, the daughter of Ferdinand and Isabella of Spain and widow of Henry's older brother. This marriage required a dispensation from Pope Julius II in order for Henry to marry his deceased brother's wife. The couple had six children, but only one daughter (Mary) survived infancy. Henry desperately wanted a male heir to the throne. After Pope Clement VII refused the king's request to annul the marriage, Henry secretly married Anne Boleyn and abolished papal authority in England. Thomas Cranmer, newly appointed Archbishop of Canterbury, declared the first marriage invalid and the second marriage legal. The political necessity of a male heir to the throne precipitated a series of events that led to the establishment of the English national church.

A second illustration was the Peace of Augsburg in 1555, which extended equal rights in Germany to only Catholics and Lutherans. This treaty mandated that each lay prince determine which of the two religions his subjects should profess. Consequently, a political solution to a military conflict dictated the religious affiliation of most German citizens.

Economics also influences religious decisions. The medieval papacy acquired enormous wealth in order to secure and preserve its political and religious leverage in Western Europe. Unknowingly Pope Leo X (1513–1521) set the context for Martin Luther's challenge to the Catholic Church when he authorized the selling of indulgences (a form of penance) to help pay for the construction of Saint Peter's Church in Rome. In 1517, Pope Leo and Albert of Brandenburg, the newly appointed Archbishop of Mainz and also Archbishop of Magdeburg (Albert needed a steady cash flow in order to pay for two church offices!), hired John Tetzel to sell indulgences in Germany. In opposition, Luther nailed his 95 Theses to the Wittenberg Church door and thereby took the first step that would eventually lead to his break with the Roman Catholic Church.

Because Faith-Belief is the Bridge-Link for Christianity, many divisions occur over theological disputes. Three Reformation debates illustrate this category. First, Luther's objection to the selling of indulgences was theological. Indulgences implied for him that humans can buy their own salvation and therefore deny God's saving grace. Consequently, Luther's motto, "justification by grace through faith," constituted a theological corrective to what he perceived as the Catholic promotion of "works righteousness" (humans can earn their justification by the performance of deeds).

Second, many divisions within Protestantism can be traced to theological disagreements. For example, emphasis on the individual interpretation of scripture has contributed to continued fragmentation in Protestantism. At the Marburg Colloquy in 1529, called by Philip of Hesse to overcome doctrinal differences between German and Swiss Reformers, Luther and Zwingli bitterly disputed the meaning of Christ's presence at the Eucharist. For Luther, when Christ said "This is my body" (I Corinthians 11:24 in Latin reads *Hoc est corpus meum*), it should be interpreted literally. For Zwingli, the verb *est* should be translated "signifies," since Christ is literally in heaven and only spiritually present at the Lord's Table.

Another theological debate among early Protestants focused on the mode of baptism. By the fifth century, infant baptism was widespread. Therefore, most Reformers, including Luther, Zwingli, and Calvin, did not challenge the traditional Catholic practice of baptizing infants. Yet radical Reformers, like the Anabaptists (who "rebaptized" adults that had been baptized as infants), argued that the Greek root word for baptism, *baptizo,* meant to dip or immerse.

Two theological insights also contributed to the construction of a Protestant climate of suspicion towards other religious traditions, as well as their own. First, the "Protestant Principle" (discussed at the end of a Christian response to question eight) warned against the dangers of turning a finite object into the infinite. Because the ambiguity of human life requires constant diligence, Protestants have always been distrustful of interpretations that diverge too far from their own religious traditions. Second, the placement of the prophets at the end of the Old Testament in the Christian Bible (see a Christian response to question six) encouraged the understanding of them as "radical reformers in opposition to the existing tradition." Many Reformers not only invoked the Old Testament prophets to buttress their own positions but they also identified themselves as sixteenth century prophets in opposition to the Roman Catholic Church. Some of the radical Reformers were opposed to the institutions of their own churches, and even to any form of institution at all. Revolutionary Anabaptists seized the town of Muenster, Germany, in 1534 and declared it the New Jerusalem. Catholic and Lutheran troops recaptured the city in 1535. In summary, these two theological insights have contributed to a Protestant ethos of suspicion that fosters division among Protestant churches today.

The final category includes cultural influences. During the Enlightenment, a foundational shift occurred in the way our culture in general and individuals in particular think about themselves and their religious identifications. Four factors are significant: paradigm shift, the rise of historical consciousness, the scientific worldview, and the Copernican revolution in thinking inaugurated by Immanuel Kant.

The first factor is paradigm shift. Introduced by Thomas Kuhn in his landmark book, *The Structure of Scientific Revolutions*, a paradigm functions as a cultural orientation map by which people negotiate the world. Prior to the Enlightenment, western Christians defined their place in the world by understanding themselves in relationship to God's story as revealed in the Bible. As creator and sustainer of the world, God determined the natural order of things and humans accepted their ordained status. With the advent of the Enlightenment, those roles were reversed. Now humans decided how God would fit into their story. Princeton University sociologist Robert Wuthnow described this shift when he wrote: "At one time theologians argued that the chief purpose of humankind was to glorify God. Now it would seem that the logic has been reversed: The chief purpose of God is to glorify humankind." Human beings are at the center of the world, and God must now fit into our perceptions of the world!

This paradigm shift in the role of religion in our culture paved the way for the concepts of compartmentalization ("Religion is just something that I do on Sunday, one activity among many.") and marginalization ("Religion is important but there are other priorities in my life right now."). Stephen Carter, professor of law at Yale University, writes in his insightful critique of our society *The Culture of Disbelief* that "religion is like building model airplanes, just another hobby: something quiet, something private, something trivial — and not really a fit activity for intelligent, public-spirited adults."

The second factor is the rise of historical consciousness. According to Luke Timothy Johnson, professor of New Testament at Emory University Candler Theological Seminary, "the greatest triumph of the Enlightenment was to convince all parties that empirically verifiable truth, in (the case of religion) historical truth, was the only sort of truth worth considering." The historical truth of religious traditions was now measured in terms of "referentiality": Does the Biblical account match the way that we experience the world? In other words, did the event really happen?

According to Enlightenment principles, all human beings are historically and culturally conditioned. Therefore, we cannot fully understand the other, whenever or wherever that other lived. Gotthold Lessing, the eighteenth century German rationalist, captured this limitation when he observed that humans cannot cross the "ugly ditch of history."

The implications for historical truth in general and religious truth in particular are enormous. Since we are historical beings and our thoughts are historically conditioned, the attainment of an objective viewpoint, a "bird's eye view," is impossible. Thus, we can never know the historical Jesus of Nazareth. We can never speak with absolute confidence about historical events, let alone eternal, religious truths. There are no absolute interpretations; only relative ones. Biblical and church authority can neither claim special status nor exemption. This Enlightenment assertion locates one of the key points of dispute in today's "culture wars."

The third factor is the emergence of the scientific worldview. By the 1600s the old Ptolemaic (geocentric) theory that positioned the earth at the center of the universe was replaced with the Copernican (heliocentric) theory that viewed the earth as only one small planet orbiting a minor sun in a galaxy that contained billions of stars. This astronomical observation created a tremendous upheaval not only in the scientific community but also in the Christian community. Since the church's doctrines were formulated in the Ptolemaic worldview (Adam and Eve were the "crown of creation"), this scientific shift displaced humanity from the center of God's universe.

With the breakdown of the medieval worldview, the certainty that went with it was also lost. The modern age witnessed a growing democratic spirit and a diminishing appeal to papal and royal authority. Biblical mandates were no longer automatically accepted. The world as described by the Biblical story no longer corresponded with lived experience. Suddenly the planet appeared unknown and undefined. A new method of consensus-building was needed, and the scientific method evolved. Instead of an appeal to divine purpose, science employed the principle of causality—cause and effect relationship—to explore the empirical world and map its tendencies and patterns.

The western world's acceptance of the scientific worldview gradually eroded the culture's confidence in many church pronouncements. Religion and science directly competed for "truth." According to science, truth statements required empirical, verifiable evidence. Yet religion appealed to supernatural causes and divine revelation that were neither empirical nor testable. Since God lay outside the boundaries of empirical investigation, the Divine was not provable. As scientists answered more and more questions about the nature of the universe, science not only encroached into the field of religion but it also reduced the need to appeal to divine authority. "God of the gaps" was born. People invoked the name of the deity only when science was unable to provide an acceptable explanation. The domain of science expanded exponentially and gradually challenged not only the domain of religion but also the very need for God. The possibility of agnosticism, and even atheism, crept into western consciousness for the first time.

The fourth factor is the Copernican revolution in thinking inaugurated by the German philosopher Immanuel Kant (1724–1804). Like the replacement in science of the Ptolemaic worldview with the Copernican worldview, Kant's Copernican revolution in thinking replaced the old theory that the mind is a "passive" receptor of stimuli from the world with the new theory that the mind is an "active" interpreter of the world. According to the former theory, a "passive" mind does not alter the perception of objects in the natural world. Objectivity exists since everyone experiences the "same" data. However, Kant's assertion negates this claim because human knowledge is always filtered through the mind's categories. The rise of historical consciousness reinforces this observation by positing that humans are embodied and thus historically and culturally conditioned.

People do not always "see" the same thing because our "life's experiences" affect our perception and interpretation of what we encounter in the world. This Copernican revolution in thinking is often referred to as "the turn to the self." Because humans cannot get outside of themselves to obtain a "bird's eye view" of the world and all interpretations of objects and events in the world are "colored" by our experiences, the starting point for knowledge of the sensual world is always the self. Regardless of the realm of knowledge—science or religion—our methodologies must acknowledge and account for inherent human biases. There is no objective point of view that either transcends or avoids this dilemma.

The confluence of these four factors has bequeathed to western culture a pervasive spirit of individualism. Many people who get involved in religion today do so in a highly selective way. Like the sovereign consumers that they believe themselves to be in the financial marketplace, religious believers of the twenty-first century decide what works for them and how involved they will become. Since the emergence of the modern age, a culture of individual autonomy has developed in which "there is no longer the idea that there is one truth, one correct body of knowledge. If it works for you, it is true."

In conclusion, these four general categories—political, economic, theological, and cultural—help to explain the profound proliferation of Protestant denominations in the past 500 years. When our society glorifies the individual by accepting a person's Biblical interpretation or perception of truth rather than the tradition of the church, and also distrusts the very authority of institutions, we should not be surprised by the dissent and division which we find among Protestants today.

Question Ten: Why Did Christianity Formulate the Doctrine of the Trinity?

Christian thinking about God begins with the specific actions of God in history that are recorded in the Hebrew and Christian Bibles. In particular, a

Trinitarian interpretation of God is based on the good news of the redemptive love of God in Christ that continues to transform the world through the Holy Spirit. Because the doctrine of the Trinity—the Christian belief that God is "the Father, the Son, and the Holy Spirit"—is a confessional statement, it represents the early church's best attempt to make sense of this new revelation of God in Christ.[10]

Traditionally two New Testament passages are cited as "prooftexts" for this doctrine. Matthew 28:19 is seared into Christian memory because these words comprise the last saying of Jesus to his disciples and are now associated with Baptismal formulas: "Go therefore and make disciples of all nations, baptizing them in the name of the Father and of the Son and of the Holy Spirit . . . ." II Corinthians 13:13 is equally significant since it is frequently used in Christian prayer and worship: "The grace of the Lord Jesus Christ, the love of God, and the communion of the Holy Spirit be with all of you."

However, these two verses, whether taken together or in isolation, do not constitute a doctrine of the Trinity. More important, the Biblical foundation for this assertion is not found in specific verses but in the "pervasive pattern of divine activity to which the New Testament bears witness." On the one hand, the Bible affirms monotheism. In Judaism, the *Sh'ma* (which means "hear" and traditional Jews recite twice daily) begins: "Hear, O Israel: The Lord our God, the Lord is one" (Deuteronomy 6:4). In Christianity, Jesus quotes the *Sh'ma* when he responds to a question about the greatest commandment: "The first is, 'Hear, O Israel: the Lord our God, the Lord is one . . .'" (Mark 12:29). Both religious traditions declare a belief in one God. On the other hand, the history of God's love for the world as revealed in Jesus (John 3:16) and continued by the Spirit (John 14:25–26) implies for Christians a Trinitarian understanding of the reality of God. This new claim by Christianity identifies the major fault line between the two religions.

The development of the doctrine of the Trinity is grounded, therefore, in two central convictions. First, the Christian interpretation of redemption (see the end of chapter 2) insists that God in Christ reconciled the world (II Corinthians 5:16–21). This assertion requires that God be both creator and redeemer (because God is one), and that Jesus be both human and divine (because only God can save).

Second, the Christian understanding of the identity and importance of Jesus created an inescapable momentum toward Trinitarian language about God. Because Jesus was understood by his followers to be the Christ and thus divine, traditional theistic language proved inadequate to express this unique relationship between God and Jesus. As the church became more and more emphatic that Jesus and God are one, a major concern emerged: How is this new religious tradition going to integrate the concept of monotheism, inherited from Judaism, with the revelation that God is disclosed uniquely in the person of Jesus and has given the Holy Spirit to the church?

This question compelled Constantine to convene the first ecumenical Council at Nicaea in 325 to negotiate a theological consensus that avoided dualism, on the one hand, and affirmed salvation through Christ (see the end of chapter two), on the other hand. Utilizing the philosophical categories available to them, the bishops condemned the unacceptable extremes and forged a middle position. First, Jesus could not be completely distinct from God with no relatedness since that would produce two separate gods and violate monotheism. Second, Jesus could not be completely identical to God with no distinction since that would nullify Jesus praying to God. The middle position, formulated at Nicaea and refined at Constantinople in 381, concluded that God is "one in essence (*ousia*), distinguished in three persons (*hypostases*)."

In conclusion, the doctrine of the Trinity, despite its historical contingency and theological inadequacy, expresses the distinctive Christian understanding of God. Daniel Migliore, professor of systematic theology at Princeton Theological Seminary, supplements the traditional interpretation of the Trinity with the following three statements. First, "to confess that God is triune is to affirm that *the eternal life of God is personal life in relationship*." God's love for the world is rooted in God's interior life of love. God the Father and God the Son share a life of love because the Spirit is the binding love that unites them. Thus, the creation and redemption of the world are the outward expressions of God's internal self. Second, "to confess that God is triune is to affirm that *God exists in community*." Because the divine life is social, this covenantal God establishes and maintains relationships with individuals and human communities. Third, "to confess that God is triune is to affirm that *the life of God is essentially self-giving love*." The good news of the Christian Gospel is that God's love for the world is stronger than sin and death. Based in the New Testament's story of the ministry, death, and resurrection of Jesus, the doctrine of the Trinity proclaims that the hope for all of creation resides in the God who is decisively revealed in Jesus and empowered by the Holy Spirit.[11]

NOTES

1. Marcus Borg, "The Meaning of the Birth Stories" in *The Meaning of Jesus: Two Visions*, Marcus J. Borg and N.T.Wright (San Francisco: HarperCollins, 1999), 179–181.

2. The subsequent descriptions are based on Justo L. Gonzalez, "How the Bible Has Been Interpreted in Christian Tradition," in *The New Interpreter's Bible*, ed. Leander E. Keck (Nashville: Abingdon Press, 1994), vol. 1, 83–106.

3. Origen, *De principiis*, 4, 1, 16 as quoted in Gonzalez, 88.

4. *Adv. haer.* 4.20.12 (ANF, 1:492), as quoted in Gonzalez, 91.

5. *Dialogue with Trypho*, 40.1 as quoted in Gonzalez, 91.

6. Bernard, *Sermons on the Song of Songs* 2.2 as quoted in Gonzalez, 96.

7. David Barrett, George Kurian and Todd Johnson, eds., *World Christian Encyclopedia* (New York: Oxford University Press, 2001).

8. Both the structure and the substance of this response are based on Alister E. McGrath, *Introduction to Christianity* (Oxford: Blackwell Publishers, 1997), 286–294 & 398–415.

9. Barrett, Kurian and Johnson, eds., *World Christian Encyclopedia*.

10. This response is dependent on Daniel Migliore, *Faith Seeking Understanding* (Grand Rapids, MI: William B. Eerdmans, 1991), 56–79.

11. Ibid., 66–72.

Suggestions for Further Reading

We recommend the following books as resources for additional reading by individuals, study groups, or inter-religious dialogues.

Joyce Antler. *The Journey Home: How Jewish Women Shaped Modern America*. (New York: Schocken Books, 1997). This book recounts the role of American Jewish women who have been activists in the feminist movement in the United States since the mid-19th century. While some of them have been involved with Judaism as a "religion," most of them have been "secularists." Thus, this book provides an excellent introduction into one of the aspects of "secular" Judaism in the structure of modern Jewish life.

David S. Ariel. *What Do Jews Believe.* (New York: Schocken Books, 1995). This book provides a good overview of Jewish belief, from the standpoint of many of the ideas which are not described in the first part of this book, but are covered rather summarily in the second section of the book. The author does a good job in explaining why Judaism does not have dogmatic answers to life's questions.

James H. Charlesworth, ed. *Jews and Christians: Exploring the Past, Present, and Future.* (New York: Crossroad, 1990). This collection of essays by nine distinguished scholars explores past and present relationships between Christians and Jews in an effort to seek a new means of communication and to strengthen future Jewish-Christian bonds. Topics include: a historical and theological overview, the New Testament, Martin Luther, and the Holocaust.

William R. Farmer, ed. *Anti-Judaism and the Gospels.* (Harrisburg, PA: Trinity, 1999). An outstanding group of Jewish and Christian New Testament scholars promotes a new relationship between Christianity and Judaism through historical study of the Bible. The rediscovery of Jesus as a Jew, against a Jewish background, as much by Jewish scholars as by Christian, shows how important it is for Christian self-understanding to reach a proper appreciation of Judaism.

Paula Fredriksen and Adele Reinhartz, eds. *Jesus, Judaism, and Christian Anti-Judaism.* (Louisville: Westminster John Knox Press, 2002). New Testament scholars write for the nonspecialist on such topics as the origins of Christian anti-Judaism, Jesus, Paul, the Synoptic Gospels (Matthew, Mark, Luke), and the Gospel of John.

Andrew Greeley and Jacob Neusner. *Common Ground: A Priest and a Rabbi Read Scripture Together.* (Cleveland: Pilgrim Press, 1996). Father Greeley and Rabbi Neusner present candid and often provocative interpretations of the history, context, and meaning of scripture. Written in alternating chapters and accessible to the layperson, the chapters reveal how a rabbi understands Christ, Mary and St. Paul, and how a priest views creation, Abraham and Sarah, and the prophets.

Walter Harrelson and Randall M. Falk. *Jews and Christians: A Troubled Family.* (Nashville: Abingdon Press, 1990). This book represents a dialogue between Falk, a rabbi, and Harrelson, a Christian Professor of Old Testament. By addressing the topics of scripture, God, Jesus, the Holocaust, and Israel, they seek to challenge widely held misconceptions and prejudices by adherents of both religions.

Carol Harris-Shapiro. *Messianic Judaism.* (Boston: Beacon Press, 1999). Rabbi Harris-Shapiro presents an in-depth study of a Messianic Jewish congregation, what motivates them and the negative reaction of the general Jewish community to their efforts to meld Judaism and Christianity. This book is very helpful in understanding Jewish reactions to Christian conversionist efforts, as well as some Christian views toward Jews who refuse to convert.

Arthur Hertzberg. *The Zionist Idea.* (Philadelphia: The Jewish Publication Society, 1997). This volume contains essays presenting the religious, intellectual and political origins of the State of Israel, beginning with efforts in the mid-nineteenth century to deal with the "Jewish Problem" in both Central and Eastern Europe up through the challenges facing the early years of the State of Israel.

Lawrence Kushner. *Jewish Spirituality: A Brief Introduction for Christians.* (Woodstock, VT: Jewish Lights Publishing, 2001). This book guides Christians through the rich wisdom of Jewish spirituality. Kushner examines four topics (creation, Torah, commandment, and the Holy One) that not only address Christians' questions but also open new "windows on their own faith."

Jacob Neusner. *Jews and Christians: The Myth of a Common Tradition.* (Philadelphia: Trinity Press, 1991). This book proposes that "there is not now, and there never has been a dialogue between the religions of Judaism and Christianity." The first part of the book explores the historical background and the second part addresses the theological reasons. Neusner calls for an understanding of religions as systems so that each party can describe fully, honestly, and accurately the religion it proposes to bring into dialogue with the other. Only when both parties grasp what is meant in context can dialogue actually occur.

Jacob Neusner. *A Short History of Judaism: Three Meals, Three Epochs.* (Minneapolis: Fortress Press, 1992). Neusner, one of the world's experts on classical Jewish history and literature, offers a clear and readable interpretation of the three major periods of Jewish history from the time of the Bible to the present. The three periods are: the time of the Jerusalem temples, the Judaism of any place (the dispersion), the modern period.

Marc Saperstein. *Moments of Crisis in Jewish-Christian Relations.* (Philadelphia: Trinity Press, 1989). Saperstein, a professor of Jewish history and thought, identifies five moments of crisis in Jewish-Christian relations: Jews and Christians in antiquity, the High Middle Ages, Reformation, the Holocaust, and the future. This book traces the gradual escalation of tension between Jews and Christians after Christians came to power in the fourth century. Because this small volume is very readable, it is highly recommended for study groups.

Alan F. Segal. *Rebecca's Children: Judaism and Christianity in the Roman World.* (Cambridge: Harvard University Press, 1986). This book provides an excellent historical overview of Judaism in the time of Jesus. Most important, the last two chapters on the "Origins of the Rabbinic Movement" and "Communities in Conflict" address the separation of the early Christian movement from Rabbinic Judaism, as well as the image of "fraternal twins."

Hershel Shanks, ed. *Ancient Israel: From Abraham to the Roman Destruction of the Temple.* (Washington, D.C.: Biblical Archaeology Society, 1999). This history of Israel is written by leading scholars for the layperson. Chapter topics include: the Patriarchal Age, Israel in Egypt, the Settlement in Canaan, the United Monarch, the Divided Monarchy, Exile and Return, the Age of Hellenism, and Roman Domination.

Hershel Shanks, ed. *Christianity and Rabbinic Judaism: A Parallel History of Their Origins and Early Development.* (Washington, D.C.: Biblical Archaeology Society, 1992). This history of Christianity and Judaism is a companion volume to the previous book. Chapter topics include: Palestinian and Diaspora Judaism in the First Century, Jesus, Christianity through Paul, Judaism from the Destruction of Jerusalem to the End of the Second Jewish Revolt, Christianity from the Destruction of Jerusalem to Constantine, Judaism to the Mishnah, Talmud, Religion of the Empire, and Christians and Jews in the First Six Centuries.

Clark M. Williamson. *A Guest in the House of Israel: Post-Holocaust Church Theology.* (Louisville: Westminster John Knox Press, 1993). This book challenges churches and theologians to become aware of the inherited ideology of anti-Judaism that has distorted their teaching, even on such key topics as Jesus, scripture, the church, and God.

Clark M. Williamson. *When Jews and Christians Meet: A Guide for Christian Preaching and Teaching.* (St. Louis, CBP Press, 1989). This book is intended to help Christians speak more accurately and respectfully about Jews and Judaism in general and the Bible, Israel, and Jewish holidays in particular.

Stephen M. Wylen. *The Jews in the Time of Jesus.* (New York/Mahwah, NJ: Paulist Press,1996). The author does a good job of placing Jesus into the social, religious and political times in which he lived, seeing him as a part of his Jewish background and not as someone divorced from the Judaism of his time, as could easily be done by merely reading the four Gospels.

Jewish-Christian Relations Website: http://www.jcrelations.net/en/index.php. The International Council of Christians and Jews sponsors this free, multidimensional electronic reference source devoted to questions of inter-religious relations. The site contains essays, news, articles, reviews, biographies, and bibliographies, as well as a search engine.

Index